To Paula —
May the
voice of rolling

WAYS OF INDIAN MAGIC

thunder be with
you always —
the warmth
you share is
best —
Teresa Van Etten

WAYS OF INDIAN MAGIC
Stories Retold

by
Teresa VanEtten

Foreword by Maynard A. Herem
Illustrations by Fred A. Cisneros

A Southwestern Arts Institutes Book

Sunstone Press
Santa Fe, New Mexico

This book is dedicated to Thomas Edward VanEtten who with his patient love believed in me. Also, Nicole Diane and Claire Marie who waited patiently for me to finish.

First Edition

Printed in the United States of America

Published by Sunstone Press in association with Southwestern Arts Institutes in 1985

Library of Congress Cataloging in Publication Data:

VanEtten, Teresa, 1951-
    Ways of Indian magic.

    Contents: Introduction--Voice of rolling thunder--Wings of wrath-- |etc.|
    1. Pueblo Indians--Fiction. 2. Indians of North America--Southwest, New--Fiction. I. Title.
PS3572.A4365W3   1985   813'.54   85-2722
ISBN: 0-86534-061-7

Available from: Sunstone Press
                Post Office Box 2321
                Santa Fe, New Mexico 87504-2321, USA

CONTENTS

FOREWORD

It seems I have known Teresa VanEtten forever, when in fact it has been just under four years. In person she has the rare talent of becoming a part of your life immediately. I find this is also true of her writing.

Teresa spent most of her first twenty years of life growing up in an Indian Pueblo in Northern New Mexico. It was then that the Mercantile, a general store, became a central part of her life. At first it was her playground, then a place where she worked and later a store she managed. The Mercantile was a gathering place where people would come to purchase, or perhaps trade for, needed supplies. It was also a place where stories were told. Stories of the ways of a Native American People. Stories Teresa enjoyed and now remembers. Stories too important to forget.

Stories, handed down through generations, somehow remain the same. The storytellers are different. The words may be different. Yet, the stories do not change. Stories bridge generations, cultures, and time.

Teresa VanEtten is an artist. Words are her paint and your imagination is her canvas. These are stories you will not just read. You will also hear and see them. Yes, even feel them. You will be there, in the Mercantile, with the stock of supplies and the potbellied stove. The Storyteller will be there too. You will feel her presence as each story begins and again as it ends.

In the meantime you will be magically carried away from the Mercantile, the potbellied stove and the Storyteller. You will find yourself in another place and time. Characters will be real. You will be with them, not on the sidelines.

Throughout this book the warmth you feel will not come from the potbellied stove. It will come from within as you accept, not question, the ways and magic unknown to you. You will experience what others before you have experienced and be richer because of it.

Maynard Herem
Santa Fe, 1985

INTRODUCTION

There was a time when reality was too sharp. The names, faces, shadows of the past stung strung together at the entrance of every unknown place or gathering.

Stories, sacred stories, told from a long ago time were told in confidence. Stories that hold a meaning deeper than words can relate — deeper than the sacred soul pumping life through time.

Beauty, innocence, morality, a biblical format passed through time by 'The People' who were sacred in the art of telling. A confidence that must not be broken is a heavy responsibility and a friend to confide in is important.

I stood beside an old man huddled over the river gathering willow withes. "There are those who were born, raised, praised, loved, helped and condemned in a safe environment." His hand reached up to mine.

"Folks have a sense of comfortable security, modest defenses and find no need to consider hiding. Hiding is a place where feelings, raw, red with cold timidity overcome comfort. Comfort protects you — no need to hide if you're comfortable. If one has worries over comfort they hide."

The willow withes were handed up to me, he continued, "I hide. Cleverness is not something one is born with, it is a tool gained from good and bad experiences. I hide from experiences that should not be shared. Shared experiences to some are terrible and horrifying.

Others grin and remark how experience makes one all the wiser."

The river gurgled and slapped against the river's bank.

"Experiences are unique, words cannot give them the needed understanding. It is true that one man's meat is another man's dog food with different taste values from one to the other." The old man stretched out his arm to slit the green willows.

"Stories of pain, disillusionment, fear, or death are a sorry note to hear. Yet, when telling them a relief awareness or an escape from these stories gives satisfaction and inner understanding to the teller."

The old man stood upright. His thin, grey braided hair shone in the sunlight. His wrinkled hand touched my shoulder. "Words of joy, hope, beauty, and celestial triumph have a tendency to worry the audience. Their feelings on such matters were never that ecstatic, perhaps the audience is faulty for not having equal feelings. Once these glad tidings are out the teller has lost them — sharing can be draining."

Again the old man shook his head. His eighty-year old eyes stared into mine. "These stories are purely fictitious. a life game challenge with a hidden source in each story. These stories are up to you and your understanding of each experience is only to awaken the awareness that the past never leaves anyone, one can never be too comfortable, *alone*."

He turned his back on me and walked away.

Early the next morning I stood in front of the old Mercantile. I was sixteen years old, working very hard in the store my father owned and trying desperately to be accepted by the people with whom I had grown up. My father had moved to this ideal spot when I was only days old and unaware of ways different from my own.

My brown hair was brushed back in braids. My ears listened to the quiet. The Pueblo was asleep. This Pueblo was mine, yet I was an outsider. The schools I went to were in town thirty miles away. We kept to ourselves, on our farm and our lives were very separate. My brothers were more outgoing. They had learned the language while playing baseball, racing cars down dirt roads, and helping with the land. I was female and the Pueblo women were a secret society.

One grandmother befriended me. She was an outcast from most of the others. When the winter winds blew she would come in early to the Mercantile and tell stories only to leave before the other elders came in to warm up by the potbellied stove. I treasured this one grandmother for she knew the feeling of being an outsider. She had married into the Pueblo and had learned the language, customs, and the stories on her own.

Remembering this, I pulled the keys up from the brass key ring around my wrist. Six locks, six keys, through the Mercantile's front door and on to light the potbellied stove. I raked down the coals, lifted up the damper, tossed in the kindling and lit up the fire.

Once my hands warmed I turned and lit the neon lights in each aisle pulling on the hanging strings that hung down from the high ceiling, moving with an upswing from one hand to the other. Soaps lit up, then soups, breads, baby foods and the cereals.

The knock was light and quick. I pulled my levi jacket down to my waist and walked briskly to the back door. 'These stories are sacred.' The phrase came back to me as I moved to the door. 'These stories are for The People, you are honored to know them, share them wisely.'

I closed my eyes remembering about the secret stories. I believed in them, I knew of them, I was scared of them. Yet, the stories are to be 'remembered not forgotten.' I said a little prayer to myself.

Our Father who are in Heaven hallowed be thy name, Thy kingdom come, Thy will be done on earth as it is in Heaven. That which hath been is now; and that which is to be hath already been; and God requireth that which is past.

I opened the door, followed my storyteller to the potbellied stove, pulled out a chair for her and sat down on my own chair.

Fred Cisneros © 1984

1

VOICE OF ROLLING THUNDER

"You are but a young Anglo girl. The sun is not up yet. Here you are working." The storyteller's face smiled through time at my eager face. "The wood stove is warm in this two-hundred-year-old store because of your thoughtfulness and the caring of your family."

She stopped, listening with her head cocked to one side. "The floor creaks with the passing of time. It is important to listen. You find the time to listen. I am old, few listen to old people. I have known you now for two years and will you listen and remember?" Her dark brown eyes met mine.

"I will remember, I am trying to learn the language." I was not anxious to interrupt her. Her presence was calm, secure and my voice broke through the feeling.

"If you must write this down to remember do so after I have left you this morning. These stories are important someone should listen and remember so all is not lost." Her voice had sharpened with meaning.

I nodded.

"This is the story of true love. A love that is only found through patience and belief. Such a love is not found easily. If you have a hard time with the words ask Uncle Tito, he will help you with the translations."

She started her story. Her brown wrinkled face spoke not to me but to the hot potbellied stove. All the groceries, dry goods, kerosene lamps and magazine faces listened. I listened too.

It is a long walk up a hill carrying arms full of corn, with the sun hot against your back, and the wind pushing you down from where you came. Powin povi pulled her skirts up with her two fingers and trudged up the hill. Her eyes teared from the wind and her hair blew wildly in the breeze. Her forehead was wet with sweat. She sighed when the view of the shelter came into sight. Her eyes were cast down as she passed her father. Her sister Tho-tu-e walked behind him. She had a smile on her face and her arms swung freely. Powin povi dropped her heavy load onto the corn pile. She mopped her brow with her skirt and sat down next to the water basket. Her sister and father had been talking again. What had they been talking about? Powin povi looked up. No clouds and the sun was brighter than ever.

Powin povi glared at the cackling birds in the tree above her. They were ready to swoop down and pick over her hard work. "Get away from here you beggars." Powin povi flung her arms at them. They flew off for a distance and then started their cackling again. Powin povi frowned and wiped her hand on her skirt. Perhaps she should just ask them what they were talking about. She pushed her long brown hair away from her face and ran down the hill. Halfway down she lost her footing and fell. She rolled laughing all the way to the bottom. Tho-tu-e and her father ran towards her. Father grabbed her up in his strong arms, "Are you all right?" He hugged her to his chest. "Are you laughing or crying?" "I am laughing. I was so tired all I could think of was lying down in the sun and I tripped. The Great-Up-Above Spirits must have read my mind. Too, I wanted you to talk to me."

Father stood her up on the ground. He let go of her only when he was sure she was all right. "You wanted us to talk to you?"

Powin povi nodded her head, "You and Tho-tu-e have had long talks. What were they about?"

Her father stared at the ground. "Tho-tu-e and I are going to the feast at Abechu-Ougeche. It is the day after tomorrow. You are both of age, but I have only one ceremonial dress for the occasion. The dress was your mother's. Since Tho-tu-e is the oldest and the daughter who has helped me since your mother died, it is her time to go out and make a life of her own."

Powin povi looked at Tho-tu-e. Tho-tu-e was pretty and very shy. She never had any suitors for she was loyal to her father. Tho-tu-e liked pretty things and worked only when her father was out there right beside her. Tho-tu-e had raised Powin povi and had given her all the love of a mother and a sister. Tho-tu-e did deserve to start her own life.

"I am happy for you, Tho-tu-e," said Powin povi. Tho-tu-e smiled, "Then you are not angry with me for not telling you sooner?"

Powin povi put her hand into her sister's. "I am only angry that we are out here doing men's work when we should be in sewing your manta and binding your moccasins. Let's go into our home and see what you are going to wear."

Their father put his hands out. "Wait. We have to bring in the rest of this crop. We are not going to leave you here alone, Powin povi, to bring in the corn, while we are at a feast. When we are finished you can sew."

The wind blew hard as they loaded up the last of the corn. Powin povi and Tho-tu-e ran to their home. They pushed open the heavy blanket over the door opening and fell on their bedrolls. "What are you going to wear?" Powin povi asked as she jumped up and ran to the mud shelves. "There are only a few things here that Mother left."

Tho-tu-e lay back on her bedroll. She pushed her hair back, wrapped it around her fingers and rolled it up. She took a long stick from her pocket and hooked her hair up on her head. "Let's wait for Father. He will show us what to do."

Powin povi went to the storage room and started mixing up some cornmeal. Her father came in and pulled his long moccasins off. His head was wet from hard work, he had a mark across his forehead from his head scarf. "Tho-tu-e, bring me my bedroll blanket, please."

Tho-tu-e rolled over on her bedroll and got up. She pulled his blanket up and brought it to him. Father carefully unrolled it. There were layers of blankets inside of it. Underneath all of the blankets were two rolled black cloths. He carefully unrolled them. They were the two sides of a manta. Around the base of the dress was a dark deep red embroidered border.

"Your mother worked very hard on these for our wedding dance. She was an excellent weaver. These shall be yours to wear, also here is the waist wrap that she started when she was waiting for Powin povi to be born. She never finished it. Powin povi dropped into our lives sooner than we had expected, so your mother put it away. Now, Tho-tu-e, you can finish it for her."

Tho-tu-e picked up the two pieces of the manta. It would fit her perfectly. All she needed to do was seam up the sides with a bright red yarn and knot the corners. Tho-tu-e picked up the waist wrap. It had become unraveled in the blanket and needed tightening. Tho-tu-e sat down next to her father. "Why is it that you never speak of Mother?"

He turned his head aside. "She was so beautiful. I loved her very much. She is still very much inside of me. I look at the two of you and I see her. She would have been so happy to have you with her in her life. I thank her for you. Her memory is still so strong in my mind that to talk of it, I could never say what I feel, what I see inside of me."

Powin povi came into the room. She looked at the manta and the waist wrap. "Oh, Tho-tu-e, you are going to be beautiful. You get your dark yarn and I will help to sew the manta. The waist wrap, you will have to weave. Father, when did Mother wear this manta?"

He smiled. "It was at the wedding dance. The first time I saw your mother was at the feast that I am taking your sister to. Your mother wore her hair down. She was grinding the cornmeal along with the other women at the dance. She had five or six young men dancing around her, chanting and singing about her cornmeal and her beauty. I felt very small. The other young men were runners in the Pueblo. They were strong and had wealth and families who had power. Your mother did not look up when her turn was finished. I heard the men remark that she had not given any of her cornmeal to anyone. It was the third day. She was there to find a man to share her life with and she hadn't even found anyone that pleased her. The line was long and she looked very tired. I thought to bring her some water, but my father told me that I must not speak to any woman in the line. The next time it was her turn, I danced around her. She stood up when the dance was finished and gave me all three of her bowls of cornmeal. Her smile gave me wings. We were married four days after that.

"She would sing and laugh all the time. She made work easy and life a joy. She left me the two of you. We did not know that she was so delicate, until after she tried and tried to have children. She would get sick. Then she had Tho-tu-e. After you were born, she would sing from her bedroll all day long. When Powin povi was born, we both felt that the Spirits were with us. She got stronger and helped with the work,

16

but when winter came, she went away. You both are my life now."

He got up and walked into the food storage room. Tho-tu-e and Powin povi did not look at each other. They were busy with their work. They felt honored that their father told them of their mother. In the Pueblo the people would talk of the beauty and happiness their mother had carried with her when she was alive. Tho-tu-e held up the waist wrap. "He can talk of it now. Do you think that this will be long enough or should I put some fringe on the side?"

They were busy with the weaving and the day passed quickly. Night fell with a sudden silence. Tho-tu-e was sad that she had to leave her little sister behind and her father was deep in thought. Would his fourteen year old daughter be all right alone in the house, so far out in the country? Powin povi was worried. No one spoke. They did their chores. The embers burned low while they all snuggled into their bedrolls.

The sun shone down on the little farm on that cold frosty morning. Their father was in the field and had let the sheep out. The corn that was special was already rolled up and bundled. Tho-tu-e had her manta on and her moccasins tight around her ankles. The food bundle was tied and Powin povi gave each of them a silent prayer and a hug. Father and Tho-tu-e were off and on their way from her to the feast.

Powin povi sat down on the ground and watched as they became smaller and smaller on the horizon. She was all alone. Powin povi walked down to the sheep. She patted them and asked them how the old stiff yellow corn stalks tasted. "No one would know but you. I shall not taste it." Powin povi smiled and walked away. The corn was neatly covered and stored. Her father had thought of everything. Powin povi went inside. She took out the bread dough and started kneading it. If the wind was not too strong she could bake it outside in the horno. The dough was stiff and her hands were still sore from carrying the corn. She went outside and started a small fire in the horno. The wind blew it out. "You stop that. I would like some fresh bread. You rest, Wind, and let me bake."

Powin povi stood with her fist at the wind. It blew her hair into her face. Powin povi walked into the mud home. "Fine. Then I shall have to go to the river and get some water to soak the dough in."

Powin povi picked up the water baskets, that were hard with tree sap, and started out the door opening. The wind lifted her skirt up and flung it in her face. "You are not going to leave me alone, are you?

Very well then keep me company, but help me." Powin povi ran down the hill and this time she did not trip. She dipped the water baskets into the fast moving river. The water baskets were heavy.

"Here, Wind, you carry this one." She tossed her head back and laughed. The wind blew some water from the bucket onto her skirt. "Oh, no you don't. You are not going to get me angry." Powin povi pulled the heavy water baskets up to her home. She carefully looked on the ground for rocks. She did not want to spill a drop of water by stumbling. She made it to the top of the mountain and set the water baskets down. "There you old wind. I did it." She brushed her hair back and glanced at the mud hut. Her home had a large corn plant growing in front of it. The corn plant was not there when she left. "Wind, is this one of your tricks?"

Powin povi looked around her. The wind was not blowing. Could the wind pick up a large corn plant and plant it in front of her home? The corn plant began to sway back and forth but there was no wind. Powin povi walked up to the corn plant. She reached out to touch it. The plant swayed out of her reach. Powin povi stepped back. Powin povi looked around for the wind, or even just a breeze. There was none.

"Wind, what have you done?" Powin povi questioned the air. The corn plant began to sway again. Powin povi reached up to touch it. A voice of rolling thunder came pouring out. "Powin povi, do not touch me. I have been sent by the wind to help you."

Powin looked around. Had her father come back for her? Corn plants do not talk. The plant began to sway and pollen spewed from the top of it onto the ground. "Do you want to go to the feast at Abechu-Ougeche?"

Powin povi stepped back, cocking her head to the side she answered, "Yes. I would like to. But I need a dress, moccasins, a man to take me, and some good corn to grind, too." The corn plant's pollen fell down on her feet. Powin povi jumped back. "Then you shall go. What you need will be on your bedroll in your home. If there is something that you cannot find, I will make it for you."

Powin povi stared at the corn plant. She knew that this was all great magic. Hesitantly, she moved to the mud hut. The pollen followed her. Her bedroll was opened by the pollen and as she stood there, the pollen wove her a manta. The colors of it were the same as the corn plant's pollen. The pollen wove her a waist wrap, and on the floor where the pollen fell was a tall pair of white buckskin moccasins. Powin povi pulled off her clothes. The pollen swayed around her body and washed her clean. The pollen tossed her hair until it shone.

Powin povi's eyes were filled with wonder. The manta was lifted by the pollen and placed upon her. Her hair was braided and then let loose to fall to her knees. She sat down and reached for the moccasins, but they were already on her feet. The pollen stopped. Powin povi listened, she turned her head. There was no sound from outside. She jumped up and ran outside. The corn plant was still there. She cautiously approached it.

"You are truly beautiful, Powin povi. Now here is your head dress." The pollen spewed forth once more onto her head. She was given a head dress of feathers. The voice of rolling thunder spoke again, "Powin povi, what else do you need to go to the feast?" Powin povi looked up at the corn plant, her hands grasped the softly woven manta, "I shall need corn and my matate and mano." The corn plant bent its leaves and fat thick blue corn fell from the side wall of the mud hut and flew next to the basket. Powin povi whispered, "I shall need someone to go with me?" The corn plant shook and the rolling thunder said. "You shall go alone. You must grind your cornmeal for four days. On the fourth day a young man shall come to you. You will know who he is. Give him your cornmeal that you have. You must be patient. Wait for four days." The corn plant was quiet and no longer spewed forth pollen.

Powin povi picked up her things and started down the road. It was a long walk. She was not sure of the way and she only hoped that the wind would stay with her and help her get there safely. Powin povi stopped at the top of the hill. She wanted to glance back and see her home. She didn't. She kept on walking. Should she have left the sheep out to graze? Perhaps the wind would drive them off. The gate, she forgot to change the lower irrigating gate. Should she go back? Powin povi looked down at her manta and her beautiful moccasins. Perhaps, but no, that would be too much, would the corn plant look after her home while she was gone? She knew somehow that the corn plant would not disappoint her. She shook her head. This was all so magical and it all happened so fast. She decided not to think about it further. She would go to the feast and dance. She would wait four days and find the man that the corn plant told her about.

The road was long and the trail at times steep. She glided over the rougher strip of gorge and entered the Pueblo just as the sun was going down. Powin povi started to look for her family. Then she remembered what her father had said about trying to find people in such a large crowd. There were people everywhere. Powin povi found the women all lined up grinding their corn. The line was long. She carefully moved around each one of them. She heard the women speak to one another as she passed by. "Who is that beautiful girl? Is she a princess with that crown? Where did she get such a finely woven manta? She must be magical, look at her glowing waist wrap."

Powin povi kept walking. Finally there was a space. She carefully undid her bundle and laid out her mano and matate. She opened the fine basket that the corn plant had given her. The corn was richer. Somehow, on the walk, the corn had dried and was ready to grind. She pulled the top ear of corn out and started to pick the kernels off. The woman next to her got up to dance. She was a tall woman with long flowing hair. Many of the young men came up to her and sang as they beat their drums. She danced around them and then sat down. She had not given her cornmeal away. She had two bowls of fine yellow cornmeal by her side. Powin povi stood up. She had never seen this dance and she was uncertain. She tried to do what the woman before her had done. It came easily to her and she frowned as all the young men came up to her. She danced around them and knelt back down on the ground. She shook her head and said quietly to herself, "I don't have any cornmeal to give them yet."

The women ground their cornmeal and took their turns until the sun went down. Then they slowly gathered up their belongings and wandered off into the crowd to meet their families. Powin povi sat still and watched them go. She did not know which direction to go in or if she should leave. She started to put her mano and matate away. She was hungry. She hadn't even thought of bringing food. She untied the bundle strap around the matate and out of it fell a loaf of bread. She picked it up. It was just like the bread she baked. She pulled off a chunk and ate it. It was delicious. She put the corn back into the basket with the cornmeal that she had ground that day. To her surprise in the basket was another smaller basket with a lid. She opened it up and there was some fresh goat's milk. Powin povi found a spot to sleep sitting back against an old tree. Many young men tried to talk to her, but when she would open her mouth, nothing came out. Father would be surprised to see me like this, thought Powin povi. In the morning, she went back to her place in the line and all the women started grinding their corn once again.

Two days had passed. Powin povi was tired. She was not able to speak to anyone. She could sing while she danced, but that was all. The women would talk about her and the young men would not leave her alone. People began to say she was a spirit. Powin povi felt like one. She was anxious to laugh and tell her stories. In her frustration she turned to her grinding of the corn. She ground and ground her cornmeal. Soon she had more than any other woman around her. When she took an ear of corn out of her basket, another would magically take its place. More and more young men would gather around her every time she danced. Powin povi kept her eyes cast downward during the dances. While she ground her corn she would look for her father and Tho-tu-e. She did not see them. Perhaps Tho-tu-e had found someone and they were already home.

Home and the sheep grazing all around the mud hut. If her father was home and he did not find her there, he would be worried. She should have drawn him a picture. He would have laughed at it. Powin povi looked down at her hands. Her knuckles were bleeding. She should stop and go home. She looked around. There weren't any men there that were different. What had the corn plant meant? No, she would stay. Powin povi was sure that the corn plant had powers and that she should trust him. It was getting colder and the wind was blowing dirt.

That night was lonely and colder than ever. Powin povi was glad to see the sun come over the horizon and warm up the world. The third day was here. One more day and the corn plant would bring forth the man that she would know. Powin povi ground all morning. She had to dance more often than before. There were fewer women in the line. The young men were trying harder and harder to find a wife. Surely the woman next to her would also leave soon. She had been watching a certain young man who would come up and dance. Powin povi watched the woman next to her as she circled around this young man. He watched her only with his eyes, his body rigid. Powin povi thought back to what her father told her of his dance with her mother. The woman started to kneel back down and then she scooped up one of her bowls of cornmeal and handed it to him. His eyes glowed with happiness. He had danced before her everyday for the last three days. She handed him the rest of the cornmeal and knelt down to wrap up her matate and mano. She turned and looked into Powin povi's eyes. She knew that soon it would be her turn too.

The fourth day was overcast and the wind blew hard. There were about twenty women left. They had to hover over their cornmeal to keep it from blowing away. Each took her turn dancing and by lunch there were only five women left in the line. Powin povi kept looking up to find her special young man, but none came. After lunch, Powin povi opened up her basket to get out more corn. She was astonished to find only one ear of corn in the basket. She took it out and waited for the basket to refill itself. It did not. She picked the kernels off of the corn and started to grind. The woman in front of her gave her cornmeal to the first man who had chanted in a funny sort of singsong voice. That left only three. Powin povi stood up ready to dance. She heard the rush of young men's feet as they ran around her to sing. She danced slowly and rhythmically to the drum.

The voice came suddenly. It roared above the others. It was rolling out like thunder. The voice of rolling thunder, it was here. Powin povi wanted to look up. She dared not, until the song was over. The young men sang on and on. The rolling thunder voice came closer and closer to her. At last, she could not stand it any longer, she held her head high. There in front of her stood a tall man. He was very handsome with dark features. Around his head was a mist of colored corn pollen. She stopped dancing and smiled at him. She wanted to speak, instead she bent down and lifted up her bowls of cornmeal, and handed them to him. The wind was so strong that it lifted the cornmeal right out of the bowls and blew it away. The young man smiled, Powin povi frowned at the wind.

She left the dance with her new partner. She would have liked to ask him so many questions. She knew that there were certain things she must not ever mention and that she would never question. When they got home, her father and Tho-tu-e were there with Tho-tu-e's young man. He was not much taller than she, but his face reflected his love for her.

Her father was at first very angry with Powin povi, then he sat down and sighed. "It must have been the sheep who changed the gates and irrigated the back garden. Also, the sheep are very good at having fresh bread ready for us." He looked suspiciously around. Powin povi smiled and said nothing. She took her young man outside and showed him the sheep. They laughed.

22

The next day Tho-tu-e and Powin povi dressed alike and went into the Pueblo to give their thanks to the Great-Up-Above Spirits. When they came out of the kiva they danced with the young men.

Her hands were grasped firmly together across her sloping bosom. the soft brown eyes reflected the open flame of the wood stove. No storm could disturb the peace we held in that moment.

2

WINGS OF WRATH

Hot prune pies and cinnamon tea bags lay on the unfolded scarf on her lap. "This story is long and very sad. I will use more words that you will not know, Nee-nee. Uncle Tito can help you if you have questions."

The storyteller swung her moccasined feet under the wooden chair and began her story.

Outside of the Pueblo lived a young man by the name of Janini-povi. He was an Indian and a great shaman. He also knew the ways of enchantment. All the people in the area knew of him and his powers and wisdom. He lived alone in his adobe home near the forest.

One day, an Elder came to him with an ailment. The Elder told Janini-povi about his wife's sickness and of a beautiful young woman who had helped his wife. His wife had gone to see the young woman whose name was Junse-Anu. The Elder though had heard of Janini-povi and wanted this shaman's help.

Janini-povi had not known of this Elder before and was cautious in accepting his open conversation. The Elder was eager to overcome his illness and with the wisdom of his years convinced Janini-povi that he was sincere in wanting his help. Janini-povi asked the Elder if he had eaten.

"No, I have fasted for four days. Also, I washed every morning and every night."

"Good." Janini-povi went inside his home and brought out some yellow cornmeal. "Go into the little hut and take your clothes off. Rub this cornmeal on your body. I shall make the cleansing preparation. Wait for me there in the hut." Janini-povi pointed to the tall mud structure behind the house. Janini-povi then gathered up sacred wood used for cleansing from under a blanket and built a large fire in the back room of the mud structure. He called out, "Are you ready to begin?"

"Yes."

"Climb up the ladder that is behind you and lie down on the blue vigas that go across the loft. Be careful not to lose your balance."

Janini-povi took off all of his clothes except for his loin cloth. He picked up four bowls of sacred cornmeal and began to chant. He danced as he sprinkled cornmeal on his own body. He danced closer and closer to the fire, clearing his mind as he chanted, "E-ai-na, E-ai-na."

Janini-povi's body dripped with sweat as he climbed the ladder to the Elder who was now lying flat across the blue vigas that lay from one side of a loft to another with nothing underneath except the fire which was burning brightly below him on the ground floor.

Janini-povi carefully unwrapped his medicine bag that hung around his neck. He screamed and fell on his knees beating at the air with his medicine bag swinging around his head. Janini-povi crept forward to the Elder on his knees with his feet guiding his body away from the edge of the blue viga ledge.

Feathers, pollen, cornmeal and herbs fell from the bag and landed on the Elder's chest. The smoke from the fire below was warm keeping both men wet with perspiration. The Elder began to moan and cried out, "Ai-Ai-Ai."

Janini-povi pulled a long feather with a sharpened boney shaft from the group of feathers which hung over his head and were tied to the ceiling. The sharp feather's shaft was put on the Elder's chest and with a loud cry from Janini-povi parallel lines were cut into the Elder's chest. The cuts did not bleed. The Elder's legs shook uncontrollably. Janini-povi yelled loudly pounding on the Elder's chest and abdomen. The rising smoke turned blue and rose up through the cedar ceiling into the dark night sky.

Janini-povi began to chant softly, then louder and louder. He stopped and the air became still. He lifted cornmeal over the Elder's face, chest, and the shaking legs. The Elder's eyes opened wide, he screamed as dark greenish blue liquid oozed out from his opened cuts on his chest. Slimy creatures crawled out of his chest wounds, rolling over one another. The Elder fell back exhausted. Janini-povi picked up the slimy creatures and dropped them into the fire blazing below. The creatures fell whining into the fire, popped and were gone. Janini-povi's face dripped with wet cornmeal which he wiped over the Elder's body. The Elder was now asleep. Janini-povi covered the Elder with a sacred blanket and washed his brow with water.

When the sun rose high in the sky the next day, Janini-povi took some atole and herb tea to the Elder. The Elder was sitting up scratching at his chest in search of scars. "Where are the cuts on my chest?"

"They are gone." Janini-povi handed the Elder the bowl of atole.

"How did I get here from the blue vigas?"

"I carried you on the sacred blanket. Now eat and drink for you must build up your strength so the evil ones do not return." The Elder asked no more questions. This was all very great magic.

Janini-povi decided to go to the Pueblo and meet this young Shaman woman who lived to the west in the Elder's Pueblo. He walked through her Pueblo to her adobe house. He was surprised to find her waiting for him at the door. Her hair was long to her knees and shone like the black purple of the summer night.

She smiled, "Welcome, Janini-povi." Janini-povi accepted her welcome, walked through the door and into her home.

"How did you know that I was coming?"

"Not through magic. My Uncle was the Elder that you treated. I had tried to help him with oils and herbs, but it was you who rid him of his terrible pain. Please come into the back room. It has more light."

She walked ahead of him. Her home was filled with treasures that Janini-povi had not seen before. She had shells from the ocean, pots that were shiny black filled with every color of cornmeal. She had open-faced baskets covered with tree pitch that were filled with oils which shone with mixed colors in the sunlight. Following her directions he walked through the low door into the back room. The windows were large and the sun shone brightly on all of her herbs and plants that she had growing in the windows.

"The medicine I work with is mostly cures for common illnesses. I also work on stiff limbs and muscles hardened from too much work or lack of care. I use liniments and oils as a cure, also natural teas." Junse-Anu held her hands close to her waist. Modesty was a virtue among Indian women and she had overstepped her bounds.

"Tell me about yourself? What do you use?" she quickly sat down on the mud banco studying her fingers. Janini-povi watched her. She was a beautiful young woman old enough to be married. Her hands folded on her lap showed her servitude, yet there was something about her that made him uneasy. He turned his attention to her plants noticing that they were of a very rare variety.

"I do what must be done or as I am guided to do. Also, I learn from each person that I work on what is the wisest step to be taken towards their cure. Magic has many forms, some are in the imagination; some are in the unseen physical hollows."

She smiled at him. He noticed her finely woven dress. Her eyes shone with a look of inner beauty that entranced him. "Perhaps I should go. It is not right for me to be here with you alone." Janini-povi stood to leave, ducking to miss hitting his head on the ceiling.

"Please wait, I am making us some special tea." She touched his arm. Leaving him to decide, she disappeared through a small door to his right.

Janini-povi turned and sat back down. The room was full of images and dolls that he was unfamiliar with. She must have started her medicine with cures for children. She did not appear to be married, her baskets were small without a family reference.

Junse-Anu brought in the tea. She spoke freely of herself and her abilities. Janini-povi was hesitant in allowing his feelings to show in front of this woman who was so eager to tell of herself. Junse-Anu told him of her parents' death and of her fear in being left alone. She expressed her innermost feelings, talking for some time. She told him about her aunt and uncle and how kind they were to her. Janini-povi felt when she paused that she was pressuring him to tell more of himself. He felt that he did not know her well enough to tell about himself or of his life.

The sun was going down. His attention had broken away from her as he realized how his presence in her home would hurt her reputation as a single woman and as a shaman. "Junse-Anu, thank you for the fine afternoon and I do hope that I can come back and see you again, perhaps when you are not alone."

27

"Perhaps, I could come and see you at your home next time?" Junse-Anu blushed, "I should not be so forward, please forgive me. I am anxious to learn."

Janini-povi smiled and walked back to the front door. On the road back to his Pueblo he turned and saw her still standing by the door watching him. He waved and hurried home.

Janini-povi was busy with his work for the next few days. The days gave him time to think about this young woman so talented in the art of herbs and teas and also in the art of speaking. She had given him an inner peace that he had never known. Her words stayed with him and he thought about them often. On the fourth day he closed his door opening with an old thick blanket and set out for Junse-Anu's Pueblo.

Her home had a thick door blanket pulled down over the opening. He dared not call out for fear passers-by would notice. He was not anxious to return home after the long walk so he knocked on the wooden door structure that held up the blanket.

"Janini-povi, how nice that you are here. Please wait for I am helping a woman with her sick baby. We shall be finished, if you would wait in here I will return soon," she motioned to him.

Janini-povi stepped into a smaller room to the side of the front door which he had not noticed in his last visit. She let a thin blanket fall over the doorway. He turned to make himself comfortable and noticed that he was standing in her sleeping room. He sat down on the floor, his legs tired from the long walk. He was not sure if he should notice her things or sit there looking at the blanket covering the door.

He listened for the voices. He could vaguely hear their conversation. Janini-povi felt that it would be best if he left this uncomfortable situation. He stood up stretching his legs, sighing with uncertainty.

The voices became louder as he heard Junse-Anu lead a woman to the door. Janini-povi walked into the front room.

"It was rude of me to interrupt your work. Perhaps there is another time that would be more appropriate to visit you."

Junse-Anu smiled and took him by the arm leading him to the sunny back room. "This is a fine time. All the work is finished and a nice visitor would be just right." She sat down on the banco pulling the long wooden prong from her hair. Her hands were colored with oil, she rubbed some of it on her hair as she pulled it loosely over her shoulder.

"You are welcome here anytime. Are you here on business or did

28

you come to talk?" Her smile was warm. The sunlit room shared her warmth.

"I thought I might stop by and see how you are, also, I wanted to see your uncle. He has been on my mind lately."

Junse-Anu squinched up her nose. "Did my aunt send you here to tell me of my foolishness?"

Janini-povi was caught off guard, "No, what foolishness?"

Junse-Anu stood up and unwrapped her apron. "My aunt thinks that it is foolish for a woman to want to be a single person and work with people out of her home. She thinks I should get married and have children."

Janini-povi watched her, perhaps she should get married. It would not hurt her disposition. She certainly was beautiful and the children she would bear would have her openness of mind. Junse-Anu tossed her apron on the banco.

"You certainly are quiet." She waited. He did not answer. "You may be wondering why I never married. It is because I never met anyone who understood what it is like to be left alone. My need is a man in medicine with the knowledge of magic healing. My aunt feels that anyone would do, but the happiness I felt with my parents was special. That is the kind of happiness I want."

Junse-Anu took four bowls down from the window and mixed the oils together in another bowl on the dirt floor at her feet. "I was left alone, I don't ever want to be placed in that position again. The man I marry has to love me as much as I love him and understand that what I do is very important to me."

Janini-povi watched her face as she spoke. The dark lines under her eyes made her face glow. She was a woman who knew what she wanted. Janini-povi thought of the women in his Pueblo who had tried to get him interested in their daughters. They were pretty, however, they had no knowledge of what he did nor were they even interested in his abilities. Their interests were only in social duties.

Junse-Anu finished mixing her oils and put them back up on the shelf. She straightened her back letting her hair fall back touching his knees. Janini-povi cautioned himself, yet the warmth of the sun and the beauty of the woman overcame him.

"Would you be interested in a medicine man who loves his art and his abilities in magic more than he could ever love another?"

Junse-Anu swung around, "Do you mean that? Is this a proposal?"

Her voice whispered out to him.

He looked at her without flinching, "Yes, I could use some help and I do feel that you are honest with your feelings."

Junse-Anu studied his face. "You are asking me to marry you?" She knelt down with her hands on his knee. "Are you seriously asking me to marry you?"

Janini-povi stood up, his emotions were great, the throbbing in his head was overcoming his ability to speak. She took his hand, "My aunt asked you to do this, didn't she?"

Janini-povi pulled her up. "No, I am asking of my own and you have been heavy on my mind since I met you. I feel there is a bond between us."

Janini-povi dropped her hand for he felt the time had come for his visit to be over. He pushed his way through the door blanket to the front door.

"You are leaving? You have proposed to me and now you are leaving?" she ran to him blocking his exit. "Don't you want to know my answer? Don't you care what I might feel for you?"

Janini-povi was tired and excitement was running through his veins. He had never felt such emotion before and his inability to handle it frightened him. "Yes, I do want to know your answer, Junse-Anu. Your uncle and aunt should be the first to know what we are doing and they should be the ones who decide if we are meant to be together. We have a power that is still controlled within our people and we must abide by their wishes as well as our own."

Junse-Anu's eyes were scared and lonely. She knelt down and started to weep. "What if they say 'no'?"

"Then we will find out together. Let us go and ask them. They are wise and will know what is best. Come with me and we will confront them with our feelings at the same time." Janini-povi was unsure of her magic and of his but he knew that the values were what was the issue at the moment.

The aunt and uncle were very glad when they heard the news. They wanted a special feast day for the wedding. Janini-povi was pleased that everyone's decision was in agreement.

Finally the day came and they were married.

Junse-Anu adapted to Janini-povi's people very quickly. She was loved by the people for her loving care of babies and farmers with sore muscles and backs. They were all eager to help her learn their ways and show her the land. Her aunt and uncle came to see them often. Janini-povi felt very content in the marriage but Junse-Anu had a hard time leaving her husband alone with a young girl who had visions or an older lady who had problems with her legs. Junse-Anu felt that because she was a woman that the women who had come to her husband before could come to her now. She felt that they should come to her. It was not proper for her husband to be alone with other women. Junse-Anu said nothing of this to her husband. She hoped that in time her husband would see her discomfort and send the women to her. This did not happen.

Her aunt and uncle came to celebrate their first year of marriage. "You seem so tired. Are you working too hard?" her aunt asked her in the kitchen.

"No. That is just it. Most of the people I could help would rather go to my husband than come to me. I am just as good as he is and in some things I am even better. He will not give me a chance."

"Is this you speaking, Junse-Anu?"

Junse-Anu smiled and pushed her hair away from her face. "I married Janini-povi because he was my equal. Now I find out that I must compete with him to feel good about my own medicine."

"Junse-Anu, your place is to stand by your husband. Not to compete with him. He is to be the provider of the family, you are to provide the family."

Junse-Anu narrowed her eyes at her aunt. "Provide the family! I am not a doll woman that is just for making babies. I am smart and I think just as he does. If he would let me look after the women and he would look after the men we would work together. He will not understand that women should take care of themselves."

Her aunt rolled up the bread dough and pushed the animal fat into the tightly woven cloth bag. "Next week is our feast day at the Pueblo. Why don't you come early in the week and help us get ready for it? There is a lot of cooking to do and you can see some old friends and perhaps if you are away from Janini-povi for a while you will miss him."

Janini-povi came into the food storage room, he pushed the flour bag into the corner so he could get into the small room. "It smells good in here, when will dinner be ready? I have a woman coming after dinner for some herbs. Junse-Anu makes the best hot bread in the country and I'm starved."

Junse-Anu and her aunt exchanged glances, "Dinner will be ready as soon as you are out of our way." Junse-Anu gave him a warm smile, pushed by him and went outside to the horno (oven).

Later that evening Junse-Anu asked Janini-povi if it would be all right for her to go to her aunt and uncle to help prepare for the feast. Janini-povi loved her and her happiness was so important to him that he wanted her to go if she wished to but Junse-Anu wondered why he was so eager to say 'yes'. The evening was spent with Janini-povi working on his herbs and Junse-Anu packing her things.

The next morning they rose early. Janini-povi carried Junse-Anu in his arms to the storage room.

"I shall miss you. What am I to do without my own medicine woman around? You spoil me with your warm smiles and your teas."

"You shall be so busy with all of your women that you will not miss me." Junse-Anu spoke harshly, however, Janini-povi did not take notice of her meaning.

"Oh, yes, all the women in this Pueblo could not even begin to understand what a treasure you are to me. You are the reason for me being so happy. Without you I should have nothing."

Janini-povi put her down on the banco near the door opening, "There I have carried you to breakfast and now to the door. It is with great love that I pay honor to you dear wife, you are my existence, you are what makes my sun shine."

Janini-povi picked up her bundle and carried it outside for her. He came back into the home and lifted her once more into his arms. He carried her out into the early morning's dawn.

"Put me down, the whole Pueblo will talk of you and your silliness. Since we have been married you have become so full of games and teasing. Put me down!"

She said this with such seriousness that Janini-povi put her down abruptly. He left her standing and went back into their home. She had never spoken to him with such harsh words. When he married her he no longer felt that he had to watch every move he made. He would always be accepted, now she was rejecting him. He liked to make people laugh yet his game had unreasonably irritated her.

Junse-Anu walked away with her bundles. She was angered at his lack of insight. She would leave him alone, that would certainly teach him to listen to her.

Janini-povi was not sure at all if he should go to the feast day. Junse-Anu had left behind the manta that he had worked so hard to get for her. He had traded weeks worth of chanting to a weaver who lived north of the Pueblo. It had taken a lot of thought and care to get this finely woven manta. Perhaps she no longer loved him.

Janini-povi set his mind back to his work. He worked all night grinding cornmeal, all night and all the next day. Finally he decided that he would go to the feast and talk to Junse-Anu's aunt. Perhaps Junse-Anu was unwell, or perhaps she was angry with something he had done.

After leaving Janini-povi, Junse-Anu had hurried to her aunt's home. When she entered the home, her aunt was in the storage room beating dough for the bread. Junse-Anu entered quietly through the door opening and put down her bedroll. She turned to her aunt and burst into tears. "I was ruthless, I was so mean to him today that I shall never forgive myself. He deserves a better wife than me."

Her aunt was frightened by her niece's emotional display. "You have had a hard time, Junse-Anu, you had to move away, leaving the last memory of your parents and now you feel that you have given up too much and he hasn't given up enough, your life will change. You wait and see."

Junse-Anu put her things away and devoted her time to cooking and cleaning with her aunt. Everyday she hoped that Janini-povi would forgive her and come before the feast day. Junse-Anu was still unsure of her reasons and feelings.

The day of the feast came. It was all to begin at midday. Janini-povi pulled the hanging blanket over the door of his home and set out at dawn. It was a long walk and he missed his wife. She may have missed him or she may still be angry he thought. He would find out when he could speak with her again.

As he started down the road, he came upon two very young girls. They were alone and unchaperoned. Janini-povi followed them noticing their discomfort whenever someone passed by them. He quickly caught up with them taking over the duty of chaperon. He found that he knew one of them, she had been under his care several weeks ago. Janini-povi talked with them along the way. He asked about their families and they told him of all the cousins they were going to visit with at the feast day dance.

Time moved faster than they did as they continued to talk and the Pueblo was full of people when they arrived. One of the dances had already started. Janini-povi asked where the two girls were going. He decided that it would be best to take them to their cousins' house rather than leave them in the confusion of milling people. He held each one of them by the arm and escorted them to the house indicated.

Junse-Anu was standing outside her aunt's home waiting for her husband. She had put on a large pot of water to heat for she knew Janini-povi would want his hair washed and clean for the dance. She watched as her husband escorted two young girls past her.

Junse-Anu stormed into her aunt's home. She had made preparations and he had gone with another to someone else's house. She picked up the pot full of hot water and started out the door with it.

"Careful you will cover me with that hot water."

Junse-Anu stopped. There before her stood Janini-povi. Her jaw set, "Would you like me to wash your hair?"

"Why are you so angry with me? I have missed you and have wanted to talk with you, yet you attack me, why?"

Junse-Anu put the hot water down on the table. "Would you like me to wash your hair for my Pueblo's feast day?"

Janini-povi was not sure if he could trust her to just wash his hair with the hot water.

"I will let you wash my hair if you will tell me of your anger."

Junse-Anu put down the blanket. She pulled it over a leather wrapped wooden box. "Please let me wash your hair before the water turns cold." Her tone changed. Janini-povi sat down and let her wash his hair. When she was finished, he sat down outside so the sun could dry his long wet uncut hair. He sat and watched the dances in front of the plaza. The young girl he had escorted hurried up to him to introduce her little cousin. They talked for a few minutes.

Junse-Anu was leaving to get more water from the water bucket outside when she saw them talking. Junse-Anu threw up her arms dropping the bucket and ran into her aunt's home. She gathered up her bedroll and hurried out of the home through the plaza passing the dancers and to the road. Janini-povi ran after her.

He called to her, "Where are you going?" She kept running faster and faster. He ran in front of her and stopped her. Junse-Anu began to cry very loudly. "Janini-povi, you will be a stone in your village. Leave me alone." She began to chant this over and over again. He reached out his hand to comfort her and she cried out, "Ai-ni, Ai-ni!!!" He held her arm firmly trying to control her anger but she turned into a butterfly and floated out of his reach.

She flew home to their Pueblo, his Pueblo. There within reach of her own magic supplies she changed back into Junse-Anu. She ran to their sleeping room and took the bear fetish from the hearth. She turned it upside down letting the yellow-orange cornmeal fall into her hand. She left their home hurrying to the lake on the edge of the forest. Junse-Anu threw the cornmeal in the lake. Instantly the water began to churn. A long ladder emerged up out of the water's surface. Just as Junse-Anu was about to step on the ladder, Janini-povi came running up to her.

"No, no don't do this. I love you, only you. Why are you doing this? Please don't go, please, I love you."

She glared at him, "It is too late Janini-povi, I-Yaa, e-ye-ni." She stepped onto the ladder which disappeared under the water's surface.

Janini-povi stood on the shore with his arms out watching her disappear deeper and deeper under the water. Great magic was with her, he was unable to bring her back.

Janini-povi stayed by the shore under a tall cottonwood tree. He sent out his thoughts hoping that she would know that he truly loved her. After many days of chanting he gave up hope of ever seeing her reappear. He wandered home.

Days later, Junse-Anu reappeared before the War Chief of her husband's Pueblo. She told him of Janini-povi's unfaithfulness. Janini-povi had escorted two girls into her family's Pueblo and then in front of her friends and family had flirted with them. Junse-Anu could never go back and live with him.

The War Chief understood this sign of unfaithfulness. There was no way that he could forgive Janini-povi the wrongfulness of his ways. Junse-Anu told the War Chief that she wanted to have a special dance. In this dance she would dance alone with another young man. She wanted the War Chief to find for her a young man who was good in the ways of enchantment. She did not want a medicine man.

The War Chief knew of Junse-Anu's great powers and picked his grandson who was also a good dancer. Junse-Anu asked the War Chief to tell no one of her plan except his grandson. Junse-Anu then went to her sacred hiding place and made her dance costume. She formed it in the shape of a butterfly.

Janini-povi was stricken with grief. He stayed at home and worked on his herbs and cornmeal trying to find a way to join Junse-Anu in the lake. A voice called out his name at the door opening. He jumped up and ran to answer the woman's call.

"It is I, Shaya-povi. I have come to help you get ready for the dance."

Janini-povi stepped back. This was the young girl that he had escorted to the feast dance. "What do you want?"

"I wanted to help you with your costume."

Janini-povi stared down at the girl. "A costume for what?"

"They say that Junse-Anu will be dancing this afternoon at the plaza and I knew that she would dance with you, so I came to offer my help."

Janini-povi gathered his medicine bag that lay on his bedroll. He pulled it over his head. "Let's go."

The girl looked at him, "But you do not have on your costume, you are not dressed for the occasion."

Janini-povi pulled her by the arm, "It is not me she is dancing with."

They ran to the Pueblo's plaza. They could hear the chanting, the singers were already singing. The dancers were surrounded with people. Shaya-povi pushed her way through the crowd. Janini-povi followed her to the front. When the people saw Janini-povi they moved back from him.

Janini-povi stared. In front of him, Junse-Anu and a young man danced alone flirting openly with each other. Janini-povi held his breath when he saw this. She was alive and she was more beautiful than he remembered her. Her costume was glowing and her butterfly wings lifted her up as she danced laughing at him in a mocking tone.

The young man that she was dancing with was laughing and pointing at Janini-povi. The young man motioned Junse-Anu close to him and Junse-Anu held his attention. Janini-povi walked up to his wife. "Stop this. Your loyalty is to me, I am your husband, not this man." He reached out ready to take her hand.

The singers sang louder, the drums beat faster bringing the pressure of his feelings to anger. Janini-povi could not believe that his wife felt this way towards him. He kept moving closer and closer to her. She put her arm on the young man's arm and glared at Janini-povi. Janini-povi put his hand up to his medicine bag. He gripped it firmly, the string broke as he held it up to her in his hand.

She turned walking with the young man away from Janini-povi. Janini-povi put his hands over his face and fell to his knees.

"Ai-ai, Ai-ai, Ai-ai." Janini-povi cried out with tears running down his face and turned into a stone in the shape of an anvil.

The potbellied stove crackled leaving us alone with our own thoughts. Dark wrinkled fingers rubbed the knots on the knuckles of the storyteller's right hand.

"There is a stone the shape of an anvil right outside that wall. Every Pueblo has one. Every Pueblo that I have been in has one."

She smiled a soft melancholy smile. "Some believe that Junse-Anu turned into a butterfly and flew away to remain a butterfly forever. I don't know what happened to her. You must decide for yourself."

The scarf fell to the floor. She reached for it. I helped her up.

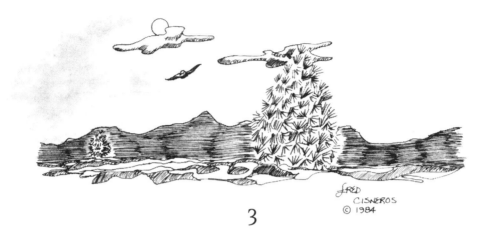

3

THE MOUNTAIN EAGLE

Two knocks and a kick on the door startled me. The storyteller smiled and stepped forward from the darkness. "You are tired. I shall come tomorrow."

I held firmly to her forearm. "Please stay."

She puckered her lips. Soft white hairs stuck out of her chin. "You will not go to sleep?" I moved her chair closer to the hot stove. "No, I will listen."

She sat down with a thud and took a deep breath. The buttons on her paisley blouse moved up, then gently down. The wind banged the shutters in time to her singsong Indian tongue. She started her story.

A frown fell upon his face, "Mama, I cannot stay here."

The woman in front of him rolled the dough out on the wooden board and struck it hard with her fist. "You tell me that you cannot stay, but how do you know these things?" She beat at the dough. Flour puffed out into the little boy's face. "Mama, it is not for me to ask why I cannot stay here. It is a feeling that I have. I can no longer stay in San Gabriel. There is a place waiting for me in the mountains. I must go there."

The woman wiped her bangs from her eyes leaving a streak of flour

38

across her forehead. She pulled at the dough. Her eyes would not look at him. "You shall not leave. Not yet. Let us talk about this with your uncle when he comes on the night of the full moon." She punched the dough.

Flour went all over the little boy's front. His scarf fell into his face. He pushed it up with his hands. He was leaving. He knew that he would not see his uncle and his uncle would probably want him to leave anyway. His uncle had made it very clear that there was no other man around who could take care of his mother except Uncle. Uncle was his mother's brother. They had both lost their spouses to a fever that came one winter. So Uncle lived in his wife's Pueblo and came for a big feast at their house on the night of the full moon.

Uncle had never approved of his sister's husband. The boy looked just like his father. Uncle could not like him no matter what the boy did. The boy would carve him a doll and the uncle just threw it in the fire. The boy would draw him a painting on dried bark and Uncle would put it on the floor. The boy did not want to wait for the full moon or Uncle. He walked outside. The Pueblo was on the horizon. He could go and talk to an Elder, but the Elders would only smile and pat him on the head.

Once an old woman who had long since died, told him that his father had once been a medicine man. His uncle's family had made him promise not to practice magic once he married. The boy knew that there were times when he could understand the rabbits that hid under the trees, or the birds that tried to eat the sweet corn in his mother's garden. He walked down the hill and looked up at the mountain that loomed in front of him. What was in that mountain that called to him? He felt as if the mountain was calling him home. He pulled the scarf off of his head. It did not belong to him. Nothing around here belonged to him. Maybe that old woman had been right when she said that he was not one of them. Her eyes had glowed when she spoke to him. He was younger then, maybe five or six. The woman had died and left a hole in his heart. She had tried to tell him of the ways of magic.

His father had been so good that he could save an animal that had been badly hurt. His father would not eat meat. That had made his grandfather angry. Meat was the main diet. One could not live without meat but his father had been healthy and lived his whole life without meat. When Father died of the fever along with a lot of others, Grandfather did not bring up the idea that his poor diet had killed him.

Everyone knew that Grandfather thought it, but no one wanted to mention it.

The boy climbed up on a little hill. He looked down at the valley. The farmers had worked hard harrowing the fields by hand. The seed had been sown and the flowers were starting to bloom. Spring was beautiful in the valley. The mountain behind him still was bitter cold. The south side faced him. The boy looked up. There were trees without leaves, deep valleys of snow, and dark shadows of winter still there.

"Juan Rey, where are you?" His mother frantically called out. Juan Rey sat still. The day was peaceful. "Juan Rey, come home this instant." The boy stood up and looked out across the land. How magnificent all of this must look from the top of the mountain. He turned and ran up to the house.

"I am here."

His mother grabbed him by the back of his shirt. "We are going into the Pueblo. I shall get Reya Cruz to stay with the house. We shall go and see your grandfather."

The boy looked down. "Mama, you can not go and leave your bread uncooked. Let's go tomorrow and I will help you bake the bread today."

His mother looked at him for the first time that day, "You will help me bake the bread. You, who will not help me do anything. Why is it that you want to help today? Are you going to take all the bread and run off tomorrow and leave me with nothing?"

The boy looked up at his mother's strong brown eyes. "No. I will not run off with all of your bread tomorrow, and I do help you a lot. Please, Mama, let us not fight today."

His mother wiped her hands on her apron. "You do nothing around here and then expect to take some credit for it. You want me to wait on you all the time. Bringing in the wood is not work, you should try washing the clothes at the river, or walking so long looking for berries and pinons that you want to cry. You just stay around here. Now you want to leave. You do not have enough to do. That is it, from now on you will be given more work to do. You start the fire and I will bring you the bread dough. You cook it."

She dropped her apron with a sense of relief and walked into the house. The boy stood there watching her go. She had a good idea. He could take all the bread and be gone in the morning. It was not time though. He would have to wait until a sign came to him. His mother brought out the dough wrapped in a blanket. She had flour all over her hands and face again. The boy carefully wrapped the bread into bundles and set it in the sun to rise. The horno was easy to light and the bread cooked slowly all afternoon.

The boy watched the birds soar and dreamed of his adventure and of what it might be. She was busy sewing and every now and then looked up at him. He moved the wood and kept the horno hot enough to keep the bread from falling. The outside oven of baked mud sent out a delicious odor. His mother looked at him in disbelief. He was working hard, or rather he was cooking the bread, but his mind was somewhere else off away from her.

She had been so proud of him when he was born. Her husband was proud to have a son, and their love was united by this little baby. Her husband had been a very wealthy man. His gift for understanding people and animals had made him famous among the people of San Gabriel. Her father had hated him for this. Her father had tried to be a medicine man. He had never had his hair cut and he practiced chanting and dusting the house with all different colors of cornmeal but nothing happened with her father and his magic. Some people made fun of him when he tried to cure illness. So her father had stopped and turned his energy into farming. Her father had always disliked the idea that someone in his family could use magic and have it work. So when her father learned of the wedding that she wanted to have, he forbade her new husband to practice medicine or magic of any kind. The boy had been their dream. He was strong and quiet like his father. There seemed to be some kind of communication that went on between them that she could never understand. When her husband died, a large part of her died too.

She knew how lonely the boy was and tried to help him with his sorrow. The only one who could help had been her husband's aunt. Then she died suddenly, too.

She watched the boy take the bread carefully out of the oven, roll it in the blanket and put it away. She remembered the day they put her husband in the ground. She had taken her son's hand and she felt great pangs of hate towards him. She did not like herself for these feelings were hard to hide. Then her brother would come and visit. She loved him and was glad to have that feeling again.

The boy tried to talk with her, but she would not or did not want to hear his words. She would have rather had his father there. Grand-father, her father had hated the boy from the day he was born. Her father felt the boy was hexed and he did not want him around when he came to visit. This brought on more pangs of hate. When would it end? Perhaps the boy was right, it was time for him to leave. He was ten years old now. He had few friends and he did not want to be known in the Pueblo.

She looked up again from her sewing. He was singing to himself and watching the fire. There was nothing wrong with the boy. He was her child. She just could not feel what she should for him. She had no love left in her.

She walked out to him. "How many loaves have you baked?" He opened the blanket and some of the bread fell on the ground.

"You are lazy, you are a lazy lazy boy." Saying this she struck him acrosss the side of his head. He fell and looked at her in disbelief. She bent down and picked up the bread and blew off the dirt. He stood and tried to help her. She picked up the two remaining loaves and hit him with them. "You have done enough. Go away, get out of here. You are a burden to me. Get out of my way, leave me alone in my own ways." He ran away from her. She threw the bread at him.

There was no bread left. She had thrown all of the hard work of the day at him. The bread lay strewn all over the ground. She fell on her knees and wept. She felt a burning fire inside of her. It frightened her. She pushed her bangs back and stood up. She wanted to hurt something as much as she felt hurt inside of her. She wanted to scream and let out all of the great feeling of loss. She couldn't though for she had to be strong.

She looked at the ground. Birds were everywhere, hopping up and down, eating the bread. She ran at them yelling and screaming. They flew off cackling at her. She was just one woman in their life. Her life was empty and work she did was lost. She pulled her apron off. The house was quiet. She threw the apron over the banco. The mud bench seemed to cringe at her presence. She sat down near the fire. The beans were boiling. She listened. There was not a sound. She sat there and watched the beans boil.

The sun went down and the sound of the coyotes in the distance caught her falling asleep. She pulled herself up and looked around. Her boy was not there. She grabbed the blanket near the door. "Juan Rey, Juan Rey where are you?"

She walked down the hill to his favorite spot. It was bare. She walked down the path to the spring. "Juan Rey, Juan Rey please answer your mother. She did not mean to hurt you. Please answer me?" The owls hooted in the trees. She saw the smoke from her house. Perhaps he is home now, she thought. She slowly walked home. The view from the kitchen window showed that he was not there. She took off her blanket and poured herself a bowl of beans. He would be hungry soon and would come home. He had no other place to go, she smiled, and neither did she. They were stuck with each other.

The fire dwindled down and night became cold. She wrapped herself in her blanket and slept by the fire. She was peaceful now, she was alone. The moon lit a path up the side of the mountain. The world below was quiet. The fires burning made a design on the earth. People were at home and they were peaceful. Juan Rey crept past. He hoped his mother would find peace and her life would settle, perhaps.

He felt for a bush. It was there. It was a feeling of peace for him, all of this mountain was that of an old friend. The path came to him for his feet had climbed this mountain a hundred times before. If he closed his eyes he knew that he could find his way to the top. His hands grabbed for a branch and he fell. Perhaps not with his eyes shut. He opened them and moved his body upward.

The houses became smaller and smaller. The smell of the fires drifted off and left a scent of strong pine. He continued up. His legs did not tire and his breathing did not slow down, his hands did not falter. He knew where he was going. The moon shone its light and he followed the glowing path. He heard birds calling out as he moved. There was a bird with white tiped wings that hopped ahead and called out whenever he stopped, or looked about. The bird would hop up and down coming closer and closer to him. Juan Rey would race ahead and the bird would jump and fly ahead. The moon worked its way across the sky as Juan Rey worked his way up the mountain. The mountain seemed to rise up to the Spirits themselves. Juan Rey followed the moonlit path and the hopping bird.

The sun rose up high in the sky. Juan Rey feeling the heat on his back rolled over. He opened one eye. Looking down at him from the branch over his head stood the magpie that had led him up the mountain. The bird chirped and jerked its tail. Juan Rey quickly rolled out from under the bird. The bird chirped again. Juan Rey kneeled and felt the ground. It was wet from the melting snow. The mud would be just right for building. He could build himself a shelter. The pine needles were wet and he could weave them in and out of a cedar roof. Juan Rey walked the area and found a space just big enough for himself and the bird. The magpie followed him wherever he went.

Juan Rey worked all spring and into the warmth of the summer. Winter came much earlier up in the mountains than it did in the valley. He worked hard gathering berries, stripping bark for the inside of his house, and he would slip down the mountain and gather melons from his mother's garden. She never saw him. He also gathered bits of wheat and grasses and tried to grind them. He borrowed some of her corn seeds.

On that day he had noticed that Uncle had been there. In the kitchen was a bright new beautiful blanket. Juan Rey had grabbed the seeds and an ear of corn and run with all of his speed up the mountain. He did not want to have to return once winter came. He made friends with the animals, and found their favorite places for finding water and food. He set a bird's wing when it fell from a tree, and the rabbits were helpful in helping him find clover.

Juan Rey would sing from morning until night. He had found a sense of relief and peace. Perhaps the ways of his father were being told to him by the Great-Up-Above Spirits. He knew that he was not to have a family and he was grateful. He could not think of facing his grandfather again or his uncle. His mother was peaceful now, and the last thing she needed was a home full of crying grandchildren. So Juan Rey sang. The birds grew to understand his ways. They would follow him and if an animal was hurt they had a call they would use. He knew it and would follow them to the victim. No other Indian came up the mountain, or if they did he never saw them or their footprints.

He gathered all summer and the winter came all too soon. The birds that should have left did not. They felt safe with him. They burrowed into the wall inside his house. They helped him eat the grain and the clover hanging from the ceiling that he had dried. His house was airtight and warm through the heaviest snows. Juan Rey felt that all of this was a sign that great magic was coming.

His mother lived with the fear of seeing her son again. She would awaken at night and listen for footsteps. One night when the night was quiet, she thought she heard footsteps coming into the house. She had then awakened with the fear that someone was standing over her watching her sleep. There were a large number of birds that attacked her corn pile, picked at her stale pinon nuts, and spread seed from the baskets all around. She had not noticed the great amounts until her brother had come. While he was speaking to her on the hill, the birds were of such a large number squawking and chirping that she could not hear him. Her brother had tried to throw rocks at them, but they were too quick. One bird had managed to take flight with his scarf that was on his forehead. After that her brother stayed inside. Even on very hot days he would go quickly inside and stay there until nightfall. Then he would run quickly down the hill and into the Pueblo.

His mother thought about the boy every time she made bread. The horno was getting old over the years and beginning to crack. Her hip would swell in the winter and carrying the heavy load of water up and down the hill was difficult for her. She thought of having a young girl come and stay with her, but she did not want to give up her aloneness. She sewed mantas and traded them at the store. Many young men asked her about her son. They teased her that she had tied him up at home, so that no one would see how funny he looked. She would smile and quietly do her shopping anxious to get home. The older women did not talk with her anymore. There was some talk that she had started practicing black magic like her father and that she had killed her own son.

She took all of this in her life as a sign that she was meant to be alone. She baked her bread, ground her cornmeal, and dried her own meat. She looked forward to her brother's visits even though now they were a lot of work. He had taken up noticing that she had not cleaned the floor, or her bowls were cracked, and that the food was the same as the last time. But he was company and a person to talk to, so she did try to make things different for him every time he came.

On the night of the full moon after the harvest, she waited for him to come before the sun set. The sun had gone down already and still there was no sign of him. She was worried that he may have hurt himself, or worse that maybe he had died. She saw a figure moving its way up the hill. It would stop every now and again and look behind it. The figure appeared to be darting from bush to bush. Mother went into the house and pulled the large wooden door shut. She had just taken off her shawl when there was a pounding at the door. She cracked it and looked out. There was her brother all wet with sweat and panting.

"Open up quickly. I am in trouble for coming up here. The people in the Pueblo believe that you killed Juan Rey. They have told the family that if any of us come up here, they will have nothing more to do with us. Father is old and he is very sick now. I have moved in with him and have the medicine man trying to help with the pains in Father's chest. I cannot be found here or they will not help us. Please pull the blanket over the window and keep the door shut."

Mother shut the door and pulled the heavy blankets down over the window. She pushed the hot embers back and let the flames light up the room. "Why are they saying these things about me?"

Her brother shook his head. "What do you have to eat? It was a fast run and I am very hungry. The lady who comes in from the trading post to fix our food doesn't know how to cook. I think that is a lot of Father's problem. Please some water if you have some, my mouth is dry." Mother gathered up the food and laid it out on the table in front of him. He ate hurriedly, stopping from time to time to listen to the silence outside. Mother did not eat.

She watched her brother's fat jowls move up and down as he gulped the food. She had worked hard all day on the atole and bread. He did not seem to notice the clean floor or the new blanket that she had woven and placed on the mud banco. His eyes were beady, and his chin dimpled with age. She had noticed the mark above his eye. His hair was thinner now and white, his forehead wrinkled and dry. He was getting old. She wondered and thought she looked older too. Now he was busy listening and swallowing. She wished the birds would come in and scare him away. He was upsetting to her and her way of life. Why had he come if she was such a threat to him and Father? She poured him some more water, "Why are you afraid to come here?" she asked.

Her brother pushed away from the table and walked over the the window. He peered out at the darkness. "They say that you killed Juan Rey. That you were tired of looking at him. He reminded you of your husband and it made you frustrated and angry so you killed him. They are talking of coming up and raiding your house."

She pushed the blanket in front of his face. "They cannot come up here. This is my house and what I do here is none of their concern. This is my place, this is mine, my husband built if for me and our son. They have no right to come and ask questions or bother me about my ways." She was angry now at him.

He took her aside and sat her down. "You must tell me the truth. We cannot let Father suffer. What happened to Juan Rey? Where did he go? We all know that no one could possibly live up there on that mountain for all these years and survive. Did you send him up there to die? Why did you send him away, or did you? Did you bury him up there?'' She looked at his feet. His moccasins were dirty. His pants were coming unsewn.

She shook her head, ''I have not hurt anyone. I scolded Juan Rey and he has decided to punish me. He had to go, he said that he had to go. Perhaps I would have killed him if he stayed. He left. He went up the mountain and if he is still alive, then that is where he is. He had to find something out. He had to go. He always said that he had to go. My boy went up the mountain and now he is gone and it is peaceful here. Your moccasins are dirty and your pants need sewing. Why didn't you remarry?'' She stared him straight in the eye.

Her brother turned his back on her. He shook his head, ''You do not understand how serious this is. They could hurt Father. Father was a good farmer and he told good stories. You do not want to hurt Father do you?

She stood up and poked at the fire. ''Father's life is his own. Your life is your own. Father will die soon, it is time. You will be alone once they have come for me. Why didn't you remarry?''

Brother shook his head, ''I can't remarry, nor can you. Where is Juan Rey?''

Mother pulled off her apron, ''He is on the mountain. He is there.'' She pointed to the north wall. There was no more to say.

Once more alone, she began to think about her boy. Juan Rey would be almost twenty. He had left her almost ten years ago. She thought of herself when she was twenty. Married, a mother, and busy being a good cook and a good wife. He was alone up there. He was not married, and probably very much alone. She felt perhaps her family was meant to be alone. They did not fit into the rules of the Pueblo or the friendship of the dances, and feast days, or the gatherings of the clans.

Days went by, and she noticed that there were more and more people walking up the mountain looking around and then walking back down. One little girl came up and asked her for some water. She said that her mother had sent her up there to look for a young man with deep set solemn eyes. Juan Rey's mother said that she had not seen anyone like that for at least nine years. The little girl played with the seed trying to catch the birds. Then she smiled and skipped home.

Mother would stand up from work and look out. There were some men walking around the hill. They were looking at the ground. She quickly grabbed a blanket and went out to them. They saw her coming and turned and walked away. She felt her life threatened and it was her son again.

Fall came and with it a great unrest. Her brother had stopped coming to see her. She had had no one to talk to for some time. She bundled up her mantas and started into the Pueblo to the store. The people moved out of her way. She put her bundle on the table and waited for the storekeeper. He walked by her all morning. As the day wore on her feet became tired. He hurried by her, and she reached out to him. "I have been here for the whole day when will you take time?" He shrugged his shoulders and moved on. She waited until the store was empty. The storekeeper sat down at his books. She cautiously approached him. "Would you look at my mantas, please?"

He looked up at her, "You are still here. I am sorry there is no way that I could buy your mantas. Excuse me, I have a lot of work to do." He went back to his papers. She rolled up her mantas and walked out into the sunlight.

She walked over to her brother's house and knocked on the door. A woman answered. When the woman saw who she was, she became very flustered and shouted for a man to come. A man came to the door, "You are no longer welcome here. Your brother has taken your father to another Pueblo. There is a medicine man who can cure him there. Go away." Mother held her head up high. "You are an Elder's son are you not?" The man looked disturbed, "Yes." She pushed on the door, "Then let me come in. There is a favor I need of you." He tried to stop her, but was not willing to touch her. She came in the front room and laid her bundle down on the floor. She brushed back her long grey bangs. "Would you please get together a search party and look for my son. I feel that he had no right to leave his mother all alone and that he has been gone for a very long time. I have been worried that something may have happened to him. He is strong as his father was, he is also good in the ways of magic. Would you ask your father and come to my house in the morning."

She looked over the man's shoulder. The room behind him was full of men. They were having a meeting when she had come in. They all heard her and they all knew that she had seen them. She picked up her

48

bundle and opened the door. "Come tomorrow, let me know the answer." She quietly stepped outside.

She smiled to herself all the way home. Now they would find Juan Rey and they would know that she had done nothing to her boy. They would find him in the mountains. He would be there.

Juan Rey had been very surprised when the bird brought back his uncle's scarf. Juan Rey tied it to the tree in front of his home. The birds kept his stock of seed and corn full. He had planted a small garden and grown his own corn. He had become good at cooking corn in many ways. The birds didn't seem to care how he fixed it, they ate it anyway. He had learned their calls and could copy them and talk to them.

His life flowed in and out of seasons. He had generations of birds living with him. His home had been too small for the large number that insisted on staying through the winter so he had to build on another room. This one had a door. The floor of the first room had become hard and solid with bird droppings. In the winter with the fire raging the smell became overpowering. So the following spring he built on another room. The birds could still call to him and he could hear their flitting in and out if there was danger.

The most danger that had happened was when a bobcat came into the room while he was out berry hunting. When he came back, the birds had worn the cat out. They had him chasing every bird and every bird was going in a different direction. Juan Rey had taken the tired cat out and put it up higher on the mountain. There were no other cats after that.

Juan Rey would walk down to the dark clearing at night and look out over the valley. He would wonder about the people and his mother. Somehow he knew that she was well, and very happy living alone with his uncle's visits. The birds brought him back ribbon or thread that she used or had dropped, so he knew that she was still there. He would look up during the day. The Great-Up-Above Spirits had a special deed for him to do. He had to keep still and wait. The time would come when they would let him know his magic.

Juan Rey's mother was startled at her work. She could hear men walking up the path. This time they were not trying to be quiet. They were arguing and loudly. She stood up from her weeding and met them at the hill. "We have come to ask about your son. Where is he?" She nodded her head. "When you find him you can tell me." The Elder moved forward, this was the father of the man she had spoken to the night before. "You do not know where your son is?" She shook her head and pointed up the mountain. "So it was meant to be. He knew that he was to go up the mountain. He was told to go by the Great-Up-Above. He is up there. I do not know for how long, or if he is still alive. It worries a mother not to know about her only son."

The Elder was going to put his hand on her shoulder when another man walked in front of him. "A little boy who was chasing birds saw you hit your son and yell at him. This is the last that we know of him." Mother shook her head. "I thought he was lazy, but now I know I was wrong. His father knew the ways of magic and he knew that his son would someday know how to use them. I did not understand. It scared me and I got angry. He needed a reason to go and that gave him one." She pointed to the mountain, "If you want my son he is up there."

The men walked away from her towards the house. The mother followed them. The door was open. They walked in. The men started looking through her things. "You did not ask to doubt me. Why do you question what I say? If you cannot find him on the mountain then you can go through my house. His magic is great, he may trick you for being so unfair to his mother."

Days passed and she heard no word. On the morning of the fourth day, a young man came to her house. He had a pouch around his neck and yellow feathers in his hair. He walked quietly up to her. "I have come to look for your son. I have three friends who are going with me. We are very good at magic and we shall find your son through magic. We will need something of his to know if we have found him." Mother went into the house and brought out his scarf. "He never liked to wear this. It was once his." The young man took it and disappeared.

The four young men crawled up the mountain. They had brought with them plenty of food. If they would have to stay the night, they did not want to starve. They climbed all through the day and well into the moon's rising. Tired and hungry they rested and fell asleep. When they awoke the next morning all their food was gone. All that was left were bird prints.

The four of them huddled together in the cold morning. They talked quietly among themselves. The tallest went out and made a bird call. A large magpie flew down and landed on his hand. The young man whistled and chirped, as the others watched the young man turned into a magpie and flew off with the one that had landed on his hand. The fairest of the young men stood up and called through his nose a loud raucous call. He called again and again. The others held their ears. The noise was piercing. Then another of the young men went over to him and the two of them together called out their piercing wail.

Down from the sky flew two large eagles. Their talons tucked under and beaks pulled up. The eagles landed on the young men's heads. No sooner did they settle on the young men, that the young men turned into eagles themselves. The last young man looked about him. There on the tree was a magpie watching him carefully. The young man called out to it. The bird flew over to him and landed on his arm. Two magpies flew up and out of the clearing.

The group gathered inside the room of Juan Rey's home. The eagle who had held in its beak Juan Rey's scarf left it on the tree where Juan Rey had put his uncle's scarf. Juan Rey was out looking for tree bark. The birds waited. The young men as birds felt a Spirit come over them. The magpies who lived in the house began to dance on the ground in front of the door. The young men who were magpies joined in the dance. They did not want to appear different.

Juan Rey returned. He carefully watched the magpies dance. They had never done this before. One of the magpies flew off and picked up the scarf. Juan Rey recognized it at once. He knew that his birds were trying to warn him. He walked closer to the house. A large magpie dropped the scarf at his feet. Juan Rey picked it up and laughed. "I will not wear this now. I did not like it then and I still do not like it."

He handed it back to the bird. Juan Rey heard a loud screech from the sky. He looked up and a large group of eagles came soaring down at him. They dove through the trees and landed in the middle of the magpies. The magpies stayed where they were. Juan Rey laughed and clapped his hands, "Are you all going to dance for me?" The eagles spread out their wings and began to screech in a chanting way. The magpies' singsong mixed in with the eagles. Juan Rey felt the Spirits with him as he watched this beautiful display of bird dancing. Juan Rey put his hands up, "What is it that you want from me, that you honor me with this dance?" The eagles strutted before him.

The tallest eagle opened his beak and instead of a squawk he spoke, "We need for you to return to your Pueblo. We shall accompany you back to your people. Your magic is needed there." Juan Rey knew that this was great magic. He watched the birds dance. He waited until the dance was over before moving towards the house. He stood up and the magpies screeched at the eagles.

Juan Rey watched as the magpies fluttered around the eagles and the eagles were turned into people. Juan Rey called to the magpies, but they just laughed and floated upward and off into the sky. Juan Rey looked at the men that stood before him. He knew that now was the time for him to lead them back to the Pueblo and it was time for him to return home. He gathered his bundles and put them outside. The men helped him carry them down the mountain. They sensed his magic as they flew down the mountain with their feet never leaving the ground.

At the base of the mountain people were waiting for his return. He reached out and touched each person that came forward. They were pleased and surprised to see him so healthy and happy. His mother was not there. He followed his people back to the Pueblo. He was told of his grandfather's death and the seclusion of his uncle. Juan Rey stayed in the Pueblo and became a great medicine man knowledgeable in the ways of magic.

———————————

My eyes traced her soft braids wrapped around her head. Her earrings swayed from her last sentence. The sun blushed a pink glow. The wind was quiet. She left that morning deep in thought. Perhaps something in the story reminded her of her own past.

FRED CISNEROS
© 1984

4

THE STORY OF MONTEZUMA

The knocks were so faint, that I was not sure if they had occurred or were in my imagination. The water boiled in the copper kettle on top of the potbellied stove. The day-old cinnamon rolls were rigid in their prepackaged tray on the chair. The old Mercantile was still asleep. The oak wood floors reflected the glow from the potbellied stove. The layers of shelves were in neat order. The wood handle poking out of the register stood waiting for its daily grinding.

I carefully opened the thick wood door. "You have been busy." She pounded her cane on the old oak floor. "You have fixed food. How did you know that I like an early meal?" Her eyes sparkled. Today her braids were interwoven with a deep orange ribbon. She did not have on her moccasins, but some black buttoned shoes. Her shawl was black with bright red roses that had long lime green stems printed on it. She stood next to the warm stove, warming her hands. She took the faded enamel mug from my fingers. The cinnamon rolls disappeared, leaving only crumbs around her chair legs on the floor.

"This story is several stories that were never finished. It is a favorite of my brother. He lives in California now. He has forgotten us." She wiped her lips with the back of her hand. She put her hand on her cane and sighed. "I am not sure where this story came from. It is important. It is also about the dance that we do. This story, though, is my own version. Everyone knows the right version, and each one is different." The black buttoned shoes tapped the floor.

She handed me the enamel mug. "Is there more?" I poured the tea, again watching the steam cover her delicate face. Wrinkles covered her face. The dark tanned skin absorbed them, as if they were meant to be there. Her nose was arched, long and thin, almost Romanesque. her eyelashes were long and curled up to her eyebrows. Her right eyebrow would arch way up and then fall, whenever she asked a question.

Her gnarled fingers rubbed her cheek. "It is time to begin," she said.

Way down low, in a far away place called Earth, a mother spider spun a web. The web glittered in the moonlight which reflected the great things of life trapped in her silver thread. The wind rustled the web and animals started to breathe. The stillness returned and the trees started to grow. The wind blew harder and a form in the shape of man started to breathe and his eyes looked about. His arms could not move for they were entrapped in the web. The stillness returned and the grass started to grow, flowers bloomed, willow withes reached up to the Moon. The spider continued in this great weaving creation and the Great-Up-Above Spirits looked down on her. They were way up above her smiling though the moonlight.

The Earth began to breathe and sigh. Father Sky looked through one of the holes in his big black blanket that covered the Earth and started to cry. He was sad to see such beauty trapped in the spider's web. The more Father Sky cried the wetter Mother Earth became. Large puddles formed and the spider looked down from her work to see the water coming closer to her and her precious web.

The Moon Spirit shook his head and from his long yellow curls fell a small thin Snake. It fell down to Earth and moved quickly through the water and found a hole in which to hide. No sooner was the Snake in the hole, than the water began to run into it. The Snake tunneled fast and found that he would have to come up, for the air was thick and he couldn't breathe. The Snake tunneled very fast and saw the glow of the Moon shining just above the surface. He tunneled even faster and shot up out into the open air. He flew into the air and then he felt something invisible cling to his body. Something which was sticky and would not let him go. He was Snake. Nothing could hold him. He pull-ed and tugged and surged with the Moon urging him on. The rain streaked down his body and set him free. There was a roar and a loud racket that followed him away from the web. He dared not look behind for he was not sure that he would like what he would see. He shot into another hole and burrowed deep into sleep.

Moon said to Father Sky, "Stop your crying. Look way down below and see what brother Snake has done to Mother Earth."

Father Sky wiped his eyes on the dark blanket, wrinkling up the sky as he did so. He looked through another hole and there he saw all the animals and trees, grasses and things that were set free. He smiled and spoke to the Moon, "Now that these things are free, what shall we do with them?"

The Moon in his wisdom said, "Let them be. Now it is time for me to rest. You will have to find a Spirit to look after these Earth creatures and plants. A Spirit that will help them grow and learn the ways of us and Mother Earth."

Father Sky said, "Yes, it is time for you to rest and let me light up the sky in celebration of this great event."

Sun came and made the morning. Sun shone down on these creatures and their plants and animals and showed them the way. Sun helped the rivers to flow, showing them the wisdom of the Great-Up-Above.

The people became restless and started to travel about. They found different ways. They began to speak different languages. They practiced different beliefs. What the Sun showed them and what they perceived were quite different. The people began to fight over what they felt was right to believe and what was wrong. Evil came.

The Sun was very discouraged with this event and called once again on Moon. Moon said that he would watch over the Earth for awhile and Sun could go off for a time and think. While the Moon shone down on Mother Earth, the people and the animals were peaceful. They got together and they slept. The animals stopped fighting and they, too slept. All was quiet when Sun returned. Sun said to Moon, "We should share this problem and if we can give them the peace of sleep, as well as the growth and knowledge of the day, perhaps they will stop fighting amongst themselves."

Moon agreed, "I shall watch over them while you rest and regain your strength, but I cannot watch over them for too long of a time for there are other things that I must do."

The Sun replied, "Then I shall also have to have help during the day. For these people are more trouble than the growing flowers, or the fast moving frothy rivers, or even the storms at sea. Wind has not agreed to help and neither will Fire, or Rain. They will do what they must do and they cannot abide with our wishes. They feel that People will have to learn on their own. So I shall have to have a companion on Mother Earth who can walk with the people and show them the way. I shall make a man. A beautiful man with a beautiful woman to be his wife. I shall get him to help me and show the way to the people."

Sun worked very hard and made Montezuma and Malinche. Montezuma was dressed in royal robes as a King and was accompanied by his wife, who was dressed in white, except for buckskin shoes. She was the Queen and he was the King of the Indian people. They were housed in a big adobe house near the Hot Springs. Daily they could bathe and talk with the people and animals that came there. The Sun could look down and approve of what he saw.

The Indians that lived close by the Hot Springs had become very suspicious of any stranger that came to pass by their Pueblo. Many times, they had held secret ceremonies for the Great-Up-Above Spirits and strangers had come in to the Pueblo to ridicule them and laugh at their dress and their dances. Some strangers had even come with harmful weapons to cut them down for performing such ceremonies. The Indians had the custom of placing spies from their village to be on the lookout for any strangers approaching. It was also their usual custom to string ropes from house to house near the Plaza to prevent strangers from coming in and to secure privacy for the ceremonies. Montezuma and Malinche were anxious to see the ceremonies of these Indian people and to discuss the ways of the Great-Up-Above with them. Montezuma was sent by the Sun to seek out a certain spy and ask this spy when the Dance of the Matachinas would be taking place. Montezuma told the spy who he was and that he would like to come to the Dance and dance in it with the people.

The day came for the Dance and Montezuma and Malinche gave their thanks to the Sun and set out for the Dance. They traveled to the Pueblo in a sleigh drawn by two teams of sorrel-colored deer. When the Indian spies saw them approaching they didn't realize it was the royal party. They ran back to the Pueblo and ended the Dance. Montezuma and Malinche arrived ready to dance with the Indian people. When the sleigh stopped there was no one around.

Montezuma got out of the sleigh, looked at his beautiful wife and said, "Where are our people? They no longer trust us. Are we now their enemy?" He was very sad. His wife looked about in disbelief. She shook her head and said, "They must be frightened of us or they would not hide so."

He took her hand and helped her out of the sleigh. Montezuma looked up at Sun for an answer. Sun just shone down on them and said nothing.

Malinche turned around and called out, "Come out. It is Montezuma and Malinche. We have not come to harm you." The people heard her and came out. When they saw that it truly was Montezuma and Malinche, they apologized. Montezuma knelt in the dirt and looked up into the sky.

The Indian people tried to comfort him and to get him to understand that it was a mistake. Montezuma would not listen he was so saddened by what had happened.

Malinche went over to him and said, "Montezuma, why don't you ask something from these people as a sign of their forgiveness as to what has happened?"

Montezuma stood up and looked about him. His voice spoke out like thunder from the sky and he spread out his arms under the sun, "I only ask that every year at this time my people, you the people that I love, dance the Dance of the Matachinas in memory of me." He put his hands down. Tears streamed down his face.

He looked at his wife and touched her beautiful face. "It is time for me to leave here and it is time for me to leave these people. Only those who do believe in me will come with me to a better place."

Malinche gasped and held his hands tightly, "Where are you going that you cannot take me?"

He looked down, "I must go away to a place where you cannot, you must not come. I must take my people and go alone." She lifted up his face and looked into his eyes, "I am one of your people. I am part of you. If I cannot go with you then I will not be." He shook his head, "You cannot come. I must go alone with my people. You do what you must do."

Montezuma walked into the middle of the Plaza and called out, "Those of you who wish to follow me and come with me to a different land may come with me tonight. Gather a little food and bury your treasures for you will not need them where we are going." He walked away from his wife and went down to the Kiva to pray. The sun shone brightly through a hole in the Kiva and spoke to Montezuma, "You shall have a white eagle which shall carry you and your people to safety away from the evil which thrives here. Malinche will look after those who remain and you shall be taken far from here to learn more of the Spirits. Do not be sad for what you are going to do shall save these people, your people."

The moon rose high in the sky that night and shone on all the anxious faces waiting to follow Montezuma. Montezuma came out of his house and raised his hands high into the air. Moon shook his head and a giant white eagle fell from the sky and landed in front of Montezuma. Father Sky looked down through the holes in his blanket and told the Wind to stay still. Montezuma carefully climbed on the back of the white eagle and called his people to do the same. Some were frightened and started to run back to the Pueblo. Montezuma called after them. They became bewitched. The others got upon the eagle when they saw the powers of Montezuma. Malinche did not come out. Montezuma looked at his house and his land, then signaled for the great bird to fly. The great white eagle lifted off the ground very slowly at first, then faster until it touched Father Sky.

The people were frightened, but they dare not say anything for fear of also being bewitched., Montezuma felt their fears and noticed that many of them were tiring and beginning to lose their grip on the bird's feathers. He whispered to the great eagle, and the eagle started to come down. The air rushed against their faces as they hugged the bird. Many women started to cry. The bird circled around. Moon shone down a bright light on a mesa. The bird followed the light and carefully flew downward and put his feet down firmly. No one felt a bump as the bird stopped. Montezuma got down. He walked around the bird looking at his people. They were few, but they would be loyal to the Spirits. He helped his people down. Here they would rest. The bird flew up and was gone.

Montezuma heard the people talking. They were not sure where they were and they were cold and hungry. It was now that Montezuma missed Malinche. She would know how to handle them. The children were asleep. The women were busy watching the fires. The men were gathered in a group. One man was looking at the soil. Montezuma looked up into the sky. What was he to do now? Moon was quiet and

Father Sky was not looking through one of his holes in the dark blanket. Montezuma walked over to the men. They stood up. They had a great fear of him. He had bewitched some of their relatives who did not want to come with him. They knew of his great magic.

The fear that the men felt for Montezuma made him sad. He had wanted to bring peace through good feelings not though fear. The men did not speak, they waited for his words.

"We shall see where we are at first light. This is a good land or we would not be here." The men just looked at him. They were too fearful to speak.

Montezuma got up and went over to the women. They were singing softly around the fires. Montezuma did not stop to talk with them. They were all tired and the fear that was in them appeared to have changed to concern for their children.

Father Sky woke them up. The land around them was flat. There were no tall mountains, as there were near the Hot Springs. The soil was dry. They looked for miles around and could not find any large amount of water. Montezuma looked at his people. They were not happy. There were also fires that were burning off in the distance. Montezuma walked to the tall part of the plain calling the men to him.

"You shall be know as Hano. This shall be your land." Montezuma stayed with them for four days. He showed them how to make mud and wood shelters, gather food, and where to plant. But, the people were forlorn, their good feelings were gone. They eyed Montezuma carefully at every word that he said. Every night they watched for the bird. They wanted to go back.

On the evening of the fifth day Montezuma asked Moon to send down the white eagle. He climbed onto its back and told his people that he would return from the East at sunrise. The great white eagle lifted him up and off into the night. The eagle flew him to Mexico and he arrived just as the rooster crowed. He went to a lake and wished that he would someday see his people again, at sunrise.

His people still look to the east when they dance. They hold their hands up, looking to the east and wait for Montezuma's return.

I glanced up at the windows. The sunshine was pouring in. The sun had come up early, the birds were busy chirping in the window. She stood up partly-bending forward. She placed the enamel mug into my hand. "You are a good listener, you are good to me." She patted my arm. "I must go and lie down. My son comes to visit me this afternoon. He is too old for you. He is too old for anyone. He thinks he knows everything." She shuffled to the door. Her cane swung on her arm. The shawl was pulled tightly around her bent shoulders. She disappeared around the corner.

5

THE BASKETMAKER

Rain blew against the thick front door. The shutters banged every time the wind changed direction. The chilling fall wind crept in through every crack in the one-hundred-year old store.

"There are some Pueblos with strict rules, we are in good favor with the Spirits. Our people do with what gifts were given them. This is such a story. The Great-Up-Above gives us all a belief. It makes us strong. If the Spirits believe in us, then we believe in a strong way." She patted my hand. Her rough palm sanded my smooth skin. Her soft brown almond shaped eyes glowed with warmth. "The hard part is the knowing of what to believe strongly in."

She frowned. Her grey white bangs lay evenly across her brow. She straightened her embroidered sash that bound her middle. She brushed her dark brown dress and settled it gently on her legs. "Life can be so hard. It can bring a person down so low, that they might feel the weight of the Evil Ones close at hand. The Great-Up-Above Spirits are united and they hold onto us tightly. So tightly that it is up to us. If we wish to fall and accept the Evil Ones or to hold on with our strong beliefs and keep with the Great-Up-Above Spirits. To be strong, that is what this is about." She smiled, looking past me, into another world.

There was a sharp crack with dark eyes peering out. The water churned and slithering tails disappeared. Willows fell from their tall stance. Moccasins crept along the bank. The sound became louder. A twig flipped up and cracked. Mice scurried quickly along. Frogs leapt frantically into the water as birds left their hunting and took flight. A soft song stopped. The slithering bodies dove deep into the water.

"Who is there?" Mice peered out, birds perched and looked down, frogs breathed deeply in the mud.

"Who is there?"

Willows fell. A path opened up, everyone held his breath. Moccasins barely touched the ground as a bright red color shone through the leaves, moving closer and closer. Rabbits hopped behind a tree. The light footsteps moved closer in.

"Who is that? Show yourself?" the woman cried. A large clump of willow fell on the ground with a thud. The tall red scarf showed itself.

"I am the Basketmaker." A tall man moved into the clearing. He was broad-shouldered and long-limbed. His hair was long with bangs cut straight across his forehead. His eyes shone in anticipation. His chest was bare and dark brown and he grasped a long sheath knife in his hand. "I have come to cut willow."

The frogs jumped out of the water, the birds started to fly down to drink. "I have not seen you here before," she said. "No. I have not been here before." The water started to stir. The little snakes scurried along the water's edge and dove in.

"Do you come here often?" he asked. "Every morning, for water and a visit with the animals," she replied.

The Basketmaker sat down. His supple body gently touched the ground. He picked up the willow and wrapped them with a long leather thong.

"You must make a lot of baskets. Do you live nearby?"

The Basketmaker shook the scarf from his long hair and wiped his forehead. "No, I live many miles from here. Over the tall mountain and across the wide river."

"That is very far. I have never been that far."

She started singing again. The animals came out of their hiding places and returned to their busy work. The Basketmaker knelt down to the water. He looked down into the brown mud. "There are a lot of water snakes in here, yet you wade in the water. Do they bite you?"

"No, they are very friendly to people they know."

The Basketmaker put his hand in the water to scoop out some water to drink. The little snakes scurried away leaving the water muddier.

"Would you like a drink from the clear water in the water basket?"

"That would be nice."

The skirt was gently lowered to her knees. Brown muddy feet pattered across the grass to a gourd. Long thin fingers scooped it up and filled the gourd with clear water. The two hands touched as the gourd passed from one person to the other. Her long black hair fell over her shoulder as she knelt down.

"The willows are very long. Can you weave them when they are so long?" The Basketmaker pulled a short willow and wrapped it with a long willow. He twisted and wrapped the willows, one around the other. Slowly a basket base formed. The colors showed patterns in the weave. She quietly stood up and waded back into the water. She sang and swayed in the water.

Morning turned into afternoon. The day grew hot and the wind stopped. The snakes dove deep into the cool water. The birds nestled down. "It is late. I should be getting back." Her skirts fell into the water as she waded to the shore. She scooped up her water baskets and placed one on her head. She carefully stooped over to pick up the other two, one in each hand.

The Basketmaker looked up from his work. "You have to leave?"

"Yes. My grandparents will be worried."

The Basketmaker put his basket on the ground. He lifted up his long body and strode over to her. "Will you be here tomorrow?"

"If there is water to get."

"Would I see you again if I came back here again sometime?"

"If you come when I am gathering water."

"This basket is for you. When it is finished, I would like to give it to you."

She smiled and turned to go. Her body was straight and the water basket on her head stayed still as she walked. Her hair fell down to the bottom of her skirt. Her deep brown eyes looked straight ahead with her long slender body flowing gently away from the spring. "I shall look forward to our next meeting."

The Basketmaker went back to his work. He worked all afternoon in deep thought. The stir of the water brought the Basketmaker's head up. The sun was on the horizon and the basket was not yet done. It was a long walk home but the Basketmaker found his way in the dark.

Days came and went. Birds flew from tree to tree and the clouds of rain watered flowers that bloomed and fell. The Basketmaker worked on his special basket every night. Early in the fall the Basketmaker set out for the spring. His heart was heavy and he was anxious to see the maiden.

He walked cautiously around the spring. He remembered how last time all the little animals gave him away. The Basketmaker crouched low in the tall grass and listened. A soft song floated up from the spring. He moved ever so carefully forward. The frogs plopped into the water. The birds looked at him creeping on his hands and knees and continued to eat their worms. When the Basketmaker moved in too close the birds ruffled their feathers, squawked and flew into the trees.

The Basketmaker listened carefully. There was no sound. The song had stopped. He raised his head to look. The willows were too high. He lifted up to a squat and parted some willows. There was no one in the spring. Perhaps he had been mistaken. He stood up and walked over to the tall tree. The water baskets were there. He held very still and listened. Everything was still. Not even the little snakes were slithering.

A twig broke. The Basketmaker whirled around. "You were supposed to be surprised this time," he said.

The maiden laughed. She held up a stick in her hand. "We had you really wondering, didn't we?"

"Yes, you did surprise me. This time I was the one being watched. How did you know I was here?"

The maiden turned aside. "I have little friends that tell me with their fluttering and chirping." The Basketmaker smiled, "And slithering." "That too," she replied.

The Basketmaker walked to the clearing and put down his bundle. "It is finished. It is very special with all the natural articles of beauty that grow around this spring." He unwrapped a large ceremonial basket. It had feathers strung along one side. Beads of wood were woven in the lip of the basket.

"Why did you not come sooner?" she asked.

"I had to work on my other baskets. I did not want to return until this basket was finished for you."

"It is a very beautiful basket and I am very flattered. Such a gift as this I should not receive from a stranger."

The Basketmaker took the basket from her hands and rolled it up in the soft blanket that he had brought it in. "This is not a gift from a stranger. It is a gift from a friend. Also, through all this time that I have not seen you, I would like to meet your parents and ask them if we may marry."

The maiden shook her long hair and turned away from him. She lifted up her skirt and walked into the water. The little snakes all churned around her feet. She started to sing. The Basketmaker sat down on the ground and pulled his sheath knife from its case. He took a large willow and began to sharpen it. The maiden continued to sing her sad song. Then she stopped and walked up to him. "How do you know that I am not already married?"

"I don't, and if you are then it is certainly my loss."

"I could be married to a King Snake."

"Well, then he is unwise to let you wander about without protection, unless he is in the water."

"How do I know that you are an honorable Indian Basketmaker?"

"Because I have told you so."

"Have you been married before?"

"No, have you?"

"Perhaps we should go and meet my grandparents. I have no parents."

The Basketmaker stood up. The maiden lifted her long hair and waded in the water with her water baskets. She pulled them to shore. "You wish to go and meet them right now?"

"It is a good time of day. Winter is not here yet, and it is early." The maiden scooped her baskets full of water. She lifted one onto her head and bent down straight and lifted the other two baskets. "Would you like to help me?"

"I didn't know if I should. I thought that you had to have an even balance."

"No. You can carry the two baskets that are in my hands if you would like to."

The Basketmaker took the baskets and followed her down a long path. The ground became harder and less green as they walked. The sun became low in the sky. The maiden ran ahead of him. "This is where I live." She descended a ladder that went down into the earth. The Basketmaker waited for her to come back up. Instead an old man appeared coming up the ladder. "Hello, my granddaughter tells me that you are here to meet us."

The Basketmaker put down the large water baskets. He put his right hand out to the old man. They grasped hands for only a moment.

"I am honored to be here."

The old man put his hands behind his back and walked away from the ladder. "My granddaughter has spoken of you and your basket. She is quite proud to have it. We have heard a great deal about your work. You are known as a Basketmaker with magic in his hands."

The Basketmaker's face flushed. He put his hands behind his back and followed the old man.

"Why have you come to see us?"

The Basketmaker looked down at the dry ground. "I have come to ask for her in marriage." The old man opened his mouth as if to speak, then thinking the better of it, walked around a mound as if looking for something. "You have been a basketmaker for a long time. You are now living near Pioque alone in a mud hut. You have only seen my granddaughter once before. You are now here to ask for her in marriage. Is that not right?"

The Basketmaker took a deep breath. "Yes."

"Do you feel that this is quite proper?"

"No, but then your granddaughter is very special."

The old man walked around the mound again looking at the Basketmaker from head to toe. "How would you support her?"

The Basketmaker rubbed his hands together. The sun was almost down and the wind was cold. "With my basketry and also, I have a large garden."

"You are both older than usual to be getting married. You understand that, don't you?"

The Basketmaker gave a puzzled smile. "Yes."

"Then I do believe that you shall go below and meet Grandmother."

"Below?"

"Yes. It is for Grandmother to decide. There are some things that you should know about before you make your decision final." The old man went to the ladder and started down. "Are you coming?"

The Basketmaker followed the old man down into an underground home. It was divided into two levels. The upper level led down to the lower level by means of foot holes. The rooms were very dark with light filtering in from small window openings at ground level which were high above their heads. The inside smelled of mint and fresh flowers. The maiden took his hand and led him to the corner of what looked to be the food storage room. There sat a beautiful old lady weaving a rug on a tall loom.

"Hello, my son. Do sit down." The maiden let go of his hand. The Basketmaker sat down with his back against the wall. The old lady had long hair that wrapped around her shoulders and arms. The Basketmaker could see that her feet were wrapped in cloth with yarn tied around the tops of them. Grandmother studied the Basketmaker's face as he looked about him. The room corner was filled with dolls hanging on the wall, feathers, and sacred snake skins. Grandmother put down her shuttle and looked at his hands. "You wish to marry my granddaughter?"

"Yes."

"Do you know the legend of the Snake King and the Water Maiden?"

The Basketmaker shook his head. He had never heard the true version. The old man and the maiden built a fire and as the night wore on, the grandmother told her story.

The Basketmaker awoke startled by someone moving. He had fallen asleep dreaming of snakes climbing all over him. He sat up and shook himself awake. The maiden was putting kindling on the fire. The old man was coming down the ladder. Grandmother was sound asleep wrapped in a large blanket.

"It is time that I should be going." The Basketmaker whispered to the maiden as he pulled himself up.

"Don't you remember what happened last night?"

The Basketmaker looked down at his feet. His moccasins were tied with feathers. "Your Grandmother gave her permission for us to be married."

"Yes. Grandfather is here now with an Elder from the Pueblo." The Basketmaker put his hand on her shoulder. "Right now, today. We are going to be married today?"

"Yes. Grandmother said that if we were sure in our wishes, we should not wait."

The Basketmaker smiled. He would not have to go home alone.

The walk back was full of new talk and heavy bundles. The maiden went right to work sweeping up his mud hut. The Basketmaker looked at the picture that the old man had drawn for him on a piece of leather.

An underground house was work. However, the Basketmaker had given his word that by summer both he and the maiden would be living in an underground home. They would work together and do it.

They worked together in harmony. Digging the hole, splitting the vigas, laying the grass on the roof, and plastering with mud and sand. Every warm day, the maiden was up early and would walk to the spring for water. "There are two other places for water, if you do not want to walk so far." The Basketmaker was worried about her long walk and the idea of her being away for so long.

"The spring and I are friends," she said and would pick up her baskets and walk on her journey.

Snow began to fall. The underground house was not ready to live in. The Basketmaker built large fires in and around the hole. He would work late into the night to finish one wall. Slowly the underground home began to take shape. As the Basketmaker worked he thought of the long story told to him by the Grandmother. The Snake King turned from a human into a snake. What was meant by the story, he was not sure. He felt that the story had something to do with his beautiful new wife. The unsureness of his future with her made their meals silent and his watch over her careful.

The day of the first hard snow came. Blinding snow fell with a hard wind. The Basketmaker wrapped his maiden up and took her down into the pit house. It was all finished on the inside. The outside would have to wait for warmer weather. He put her down near the large fireplace with the fire burning.

"Basketmaker, you have made a warm home out of a mud basket," the maiden laughed. "Now we can hang all of your baskets in this big mud basket." The Basketmaker smiled. He pulled up his blanket. There were all the bedrolls to bring through the wind and snow. "You stay here and I'll bring our belongings. We better just stay here for the winter. Here we have two warm rooms and that mud hut doesn't even keep the caterpillars warm."

"I'll unpack what you bring."

The Basketmaker went up the footholes and out into the blizzard. The maiden swept the floor, put the bundle of willows in the corner, and pushed the straw into the corner for their bed.

The winter months passed. The Basketmaker worked on his baskets and the maiden worked on weaving blankets. The Basketmaker settled down to his life with his beautiful woman. He tried not to think of the grandmother's story. The warmth of their pit house kept out all bad spirits. Their life was alone with no outsiders coming or going. The plants the maiden grew in pots by the fireplace and the window opening started to grow green leaves.

Winter passed into spring. A spring that would not make up its mind. The Basketmaker shed his heavy clothing. The maiden laughed with joy when the birds started pecking at the window opening. "They want to come in. They know that life is growing in here."

The Basketmaker walked over to the window. "Now can I ask why you are so fat?"

The maiden laughed and pushed him away from her. "We have been alone all winter, but we will not be alone this summer." She took his hand and placed it on her belly. She was large with child. The child was kicking and pushing. "Soon your child will want to see the sunshine and watch you make baskets."

The Basketmaker picked her up in his arms. "You are such a joy. How could I ever worry about us." He put her down. He walked over to the footholes, gathering all his baskets. "I must go into town and trade the baskets for food and clothing." He pulled a blanket around his finely woven baskets. The maiden helped him tie them to his back. She pushed him up the ladder.

"I shall be back before dark. Perhaps this basketmaker can bring his woman back a present."

The maiden quickly gathered the water baskets and walked out to the spring. The weather was warm in the morning but as the day wore on the cold winds started to blow. The maiden walked back to the pit house. She was chilled and her moccasins were wet. She built a fire and waited for the Basketmaker. She was very cold and the fire did not seem to warm her. She pulled herself up under a thick blanket and fell asleep on the straw bed. The sun started to go down. The clouds also grew in their way and a light snow started to fall.

The Basketmaker hurried on his way. He reached the ladder as the sun tipped over the edge of the mountain. "I am home with good news. The store gave us some presents. They didn't even know that we were married." He jumped down the foothole ledge to the ground floor. He turned to look for his wife. She was not there. He put down his heavy blanket and knelt on the floor to unpack it. He stopped and lifted his head high. There was a sound. A very strange sound. He slowly turned and looked at what was coming up behind him. The

Basketmaker stood up, his hands over his eyes. "No, no, no, no, this cannot be. I am a father and then I am a man without a wife on the same day."

The Basketmaker turned and went up the footholes. He sat down on the ledge and shook his head. There down below him was a snake. "A snake. Your grandmother told me, she warned me. I never thought that this would really happen. I love you. I love you as a woman, my woman. Now you are a snake. The Spirits will help us. You shall not remain a snake. Can you talk to me?" The snake hissed below. Her colors glowed in the firelight. "You are of the same coloring as the little snakes in the spring, you are so large. Is that because you are still carrying my child?"

The snake hissed below him. The Basketmaker leaned back against the wall. His mind was full of questions. The snow fell and as the night wore on, the snow began to stay on the ground. Slowly the Basketmaker climbed down the footholes. The snake lay curled up in front of the dying fire. The Basketmaker put logs on the fire. He walked very carefully over to the blanket roll he had brought home. He carefully unrolled it all the way. There were three baskets that he had to change. The jerky, cornmeal and peppermints, he lifted up to the shelf. He then pulled out a small blanket and placed it in front of the snake. She hissed at him. The light from the fire showed her fangs.

"So you are not only a snake, but you are poisonous as well. Do not worry, I shall never harm you. Let me open your present for you. If this is the way it must be, then, I shall learn to live with it." He opened the blanket. There shining in the glowing light was a delicate silver concha shell. The Basketmaker laid it out on the floor in front of the snake. The snake coiled up and hissed. "Well, I'll put it away. Perhaps you are hungry."

The Basketmaker rolled up the concha shell in a cloth and put it up on a shelf. He took down the largest basket that he had made and laid it down in front of the fire. The snake crawled into it. The blanket, he wrapped around the outside of the basket. The Basketmaker stood up and looked around him. "What do snakes eat?" The Basketmaker shook his head. He climbed up the footholes and put on his heavy blanket. He climbed out into the night.

The Basketmaker found that snakes like mud with little animals in it. Sometimes if he was real still while cutting willows he could catch a mouse. The Basketmaker decided that his life should be as normal as

70

he could make it. He left the snake alone except to feed her. She hissed at him. The fangs were large and his fear of her was enough to keep him outside during the summer months. She was growing larger and larger each day. He had not been able to speak to his wife about the time the child was due. This was all very great magic.

"Would you like to go outside today, to the spring?" The snake would hiss and curl up in the basket. He left her alone and went on his way. He wove his baskets on the ledge at night. Once a month, he would go into town and trade for food. The ladies of the Pueblo were anxious to meet his wife. He never said anything, one way or the other.

"The nights are growing cool again. I must go out and get firewood. I have left you two baskets with mud, and one large basket with water. My bedroll is packed and I shall be gone for two or three days. Be careful of strangers. I shall lower the ladder. Good-bye." He reached out to touch her. She did not hiss. He touched her gently with his fingers. Her skin was cold. She had been a snake through the spring and now the summer was passing. He stood up and grabbed his bedroll. "Good-bye."

The ladies from the Pueblo decided that the time had come for them to meet the Basketmaker's wife. He had come in the spring happy with the news of his child coming. Certainly his wife must need some help and some teaching of the way to have children. They packed food, clothing, and bread and started off. They walked full of good feeling. When they reached the mud hut, it was deserted and fallen in. They walked around to the side of the mud hut. "Look there is a window opening going down into the ground. Let's see what is down there."

The ladies all huddled around the window opening, blocking the sunshine from entering the underground home. The snake moved out of the basket and crawled toward the window opening. The ladies all gasped and rushed away. They walked around and found a hole that went down into the earth. There was no way to enter the hole.

"The Basketmaker and his wife must have gone for wood. The ladder is gone and his woodpile is low. Perhaps he keeps a snake for a pet." "Where do they live?" "They must live down there. The hut is a mess. The Basketmaker made a house to look like a mud basket." They all laughed. The ladies looked around for a stick to lower their presents down into the underground home. "Let us just go home and have another journey out when they get back."

The ladies all wrapped their blankets around themselves and hurried back to the Pueblo giggling with the news of a snake in the Basketmaker's house.

The nights were cold, the days warm, the Basketmaker gathered his wood in two days time. He walked home slowly. His spirit was sad. The underground home looked empty from the distance. Empty, barely with life. He pulled his wood up to the hole. He knelt down and listened. There was no sound. Perhaps she was asleep. He thought of her perhaps turning back into his wife again. He shook his head grabbed the sides of the hole and jumped down. There it was. She was hissing. She was still a snake. He picked up the ladder and lifted it to the top opening. He went up the hole and dropped down the wood. He stacked it on the ledge. He did not want to look at her or be with her as a snake. He unloaded all the wood. He climbed the ladder to put the large pieces of wood away. There were footprints around the window. He followed them to the opening. Then he saw where they had turned back to the Pueblo.

He jumped down the hole to look for any human signs. Carefully, he worked his way down the footholes. It was dark. He had forgotten how dark the underground home was without a fire. He moved his feet gently, she was hissing louder. The Basketmaker leaned over the fireplace. He stirred the ashes, laid down the kindling and firewood. He rubbed his flint and lit the fire. He stared into the fire and felt its warmth. The snake was now quiet. The Basketmaker crawled over to the straw bed and fell asleep.

The sunshine on the floor brought about a great stirring in the morning. The Basketmaker turned and looked to the wall. He closed his eyes. His back hurt, his hands were sore, and he was tired. He felt something crawl up his leg. He didn't move. Something was crawling over his pillow, while the thing on his leg fell on the floor with a thud. The Basketmaker gently lifted his head. His neck was burning with stiffness. He turned and sat up. The snake was hissing by the fire. The floor, bed, baskets, and shelves were full of little snakes. She had her children. The Basketmaker felt the tears roll off his cheek onto his hand. He pulled himself up.

"You had your children while I was gone? All by yourself? I must go out and bring them food, you also must be hungry." He picked up his moccasins. There was a little snake crawling in the bottom. The

Basketmaker smiled. "You're too little to wear my moccasin." He carefully put the little snake on the floor. The mother snake slithered over to him and hissed. "I wouldn't hurt the little snake. He is mine too."

The Basketmaker pulled on his old blanket and scarf and went out to the spring. The frogs still jumped, the birds chirped, and the little water snakes slithered away from him as he dug deep into the mud. He caught up a little snake in one of the baskets. "You cannot come home with me. I have enough of you in my house without another." He tipped the basket over and the snake disappeared in the spring.

The Basketmaker had to make two trips to the spring. Each time he walked up he remembered how beautiful his wife had been, singing and swaying in the water. His spirit was strengthened by the memory of the way she used to be. "Here you go little ones. Your first mud. Mother better show you how to eat."

Days, months passed. The little snakes grew. The Basketmaker was comfortable with their slithering around. He now slept up on the ledge above them. As they grew, they were becoming poisonous like their mother. He did not want to roll on top of one in his sleep. His baskets grew in number and it was time for him to take them to town to trade. He gathered them up in his blanket and lifted it on to his back. His eye caught the small blanket on the shelf. Her concha shell would wait. It was his first present to her. He leaned down the ledge. "I will be back before dark. I am taking some baskets and you will have fresh mud for dinner. If this is the way it must be, I will just have to live with it."

The Basketmaker spent more time in the Pueblo than he had meant to. The old men were telling stories and the ladies were cooking up fry bread. The Basketmaker gathered up his bundle and started home. The people in the Pueblo were anxious to meet his wife. They joked about him hiding her away. His head was full of wonder at the full moon that came up before dark. The Basketmaker walked to the spring. He put down the baskets. His feet were tired. He leaned against the tree in the clearing.

The sunshine woke him with a start. He had been at the spring all night. The snakes must be very hungry without a dinner and now without a breakfast. He jumped up and gathered the baskets full of mud. He pulled his blanket roll over his shoulders and started·for home. His eyes looked down to avoid the glare from the sun. He almost tripped over the baskets that were lined up next to the ladder on the ground. The Basketmaker put down the mud. He looked at the baskets. Each basket had the almost full grown snakes in them. He looked around. "Hello. Is there anyone here? What are you doing with my snakes?"

The Basketmaker walked around the ladder. There were no footprints only snake markings on the dirt. He turned quickly. There in front of him was the mother snake. She was hissing loudly. In front of each basket she had formed an arrow. "Do you want me to take the snakes away?" She swayed her head in a motion. The Basketmaker knelt down to her. Her fangs were gone. "Do you want me to take these snakes to water? Each basket in the direction of the arrow?" The mother snake nodded. The Basketmaker went to the first basket. The arrow pointed east. He lifted it up to his shoulder and walked to the river. He put the basket down. They tipped it over and slithered into the deep mud.

The Basketmaker returned and took the next basket to the west. Then he took one to the north and another to the south. The arrows all pointed away from the spring. He walked into the night to deliver the last basket to the spring that was down in the flat lands. Water was hard to find. When he returned, smoke was coming out of the fire hole. The Basketmaker held his breath as he touched the ladder. Suppose she is now a woman. She may still be a snake. He quietly climbed down the ladder to the ledge. He looked down below him. There were piles of mud all over the floor. The blankets were strewn from wall to wall. The odor was strong. He tilted his head and listened. There was no sound.

"Hello, are you there?" Suddenly, something grabbed him around the waist. He turned and looked into the face of his wife. "You broke the spell. You stayed with me and never wished me dead. You fed us and looked after us. You followed the directions that the Great-Up-Above Spirits told me to give you. We have broken the enchantment."

The Basketmaker followed her down the footholes. A spider's web clung to the roof of the underground ceiling and draped down to the ground floor. "That is how you got the snakes out." He pointed to the web. The maiden shook her head. "It is over. Let us not talk about it again. We have our life to live now." The Basketmaker reached for the blanket on the shelf. He handed it to her. The blanket glowed in her hands. She unrolled it and pulled out the silver concha shell.

The Basketmaker went to the Pueblo and asked if he could present his wife to the Pueblo at a dance. The Elders agreed. The Basketmaker took his wife to the Pueblo and introduced her to the Elders. After they had met her, she was taken to the center of the Pueblo. Each family came up and met her. They gave her a basket and danced with her. Her beauty shone clearly to all who met her.

Her hand went forward grasping something that wasn't there. She smiled showing three ragged front teeth. The beauty in the story had transferred itself to her. She looked into my eyes, capturing my senses, mingling them with hers, and returning them back to me.

The room was still dark. The large store had heard many tales told, yet, in the dark dawn, it was in awe of this woman. The magic of her voice, whispering at times, then shy, and almost loud, telling of the beauty and the love that people had felt for each other.

Her hand was still outstretched. Her eyes were watering. Perhaps she had known the snake and the woman. Perhaps, she had known the man. She dropped her hand into her lap. The life had escaped from her. She moved her foot under the chair and lifted herself up. We did not speak. We felt each other's warmth in a short embrace. She shuffled to the door and was gone.

CISNEROS
© 1984

6

SAI-YA

The next morning was bitter cold. Snow had fallen in the night. The world had grown old in its white slumber. The knocks and kick were sharp and forceful. The woman was bent and worn. Her gnarled arthritic fingers groped at the layers of shawls around her shoulders. The black rubbers were white from the ankle down.

She shuffled slowly to the chair. The tea steam drifted up around her nostrils. Her hands shook as she lifted the cup to her lips. "You are a good listener. Do not forget for no one can tell you what has happened." She nodded forward toward the door. We sat in silence. The potbellied stove quietly warmed the large room. The floor creaked and groaned. The old lady was tired. Her fingers hugged the warm enamel mug. She was slowly warming up. Her shivering was less obvious.

The knowledge of the stories was deep in her mind. I sat and thought about the people who must have told her these stories. They were from a long time ago. They, too, must have told her that she was a good listener. The stories did seem to differ in temperament. Perhaps different people had told her the stories.

She sighed and hugged her chest. She glanced at me. I knew not to speak. Her body was frail and small, the stories were large and fulfilling. She relaxed and put her shoulders back. "This story is my favorite. I will tell it to you, you can close your eyes and see the colors that appear in the clear skies of long ago.

The flowers bloomed and opened up to the bright sunlight. The hills rolled in their morning exercise. The earth moved, plants stretched and rabbits hopped away. The ground lifted up. Mother Earth groaned, pushing hard, as a figure grew out from the soft brown dirt. A tall figure rose up. The tall figure took shape, long hair blew in the wind. Dark brown arms reached out toward Father Sky. The rain from the night before had brought about the birth of a maiden. Her legs still forming pulled out of the dirt to move and walk. "Sai-ya, ya, ya, ya." She called up to Father Sky. The sun shone brightly down on her. The hot rays hardened her limbs and tanned her face. Her legs grew and at last her feet danced her away from the place of her birth. Her fingers groped for life and her arms anxious to reach flung out to grasp the world. She turned around and around. The air churned about her, a manta covered her body, moccasins of white covered her feet. She turned less and less and stopped. On her arms were bracelets of turquoise and silver. Her necklace was of soft silver beads, and her waist wrapped in concha shaped silver ovals with stones of blue color in them. "I am free," she called.

She walked towards the mesa to look over the land. She looked up into the sky and saw a large eagle flying towards her. His claws stretched out, he was coming down for the kill. She put out her hand, yelling at the bird. The bird fell on top of her, his claws in her back. She twisted and fought for her freedom. His talons held her through the muscle in her back. The bird lifted her off the ground and carried her over the mesa and into the mountains. The maiden cried out. "Sai-ya, ya, ya."

The bird tightened his grip. Blood dripped from her back. She pulled her manta to hold herself up and to keep from falling. The bird soared higher. He flew against the side of a canyon. A river raged below them. The wind thrust itself against her, she became a puppet above her Mother Earth. Blood fell from her nose, eyes, and mouth. Her head fell forward and her limbs went limp. The eagle soared looking up at the sun. He flew across the mountains, plains and river lands. The sun went down and the moon rose. The moon's fierce yellow face shone firmly down on the eagle. The eagle became weak. His wings became heavy and his strength gave out. He flew down, down, down to earth.

Mother Earth opened her arms to catch her creation. The eagle fell. The maiden unaware of her captor fell with him. They fell at a great speed. The eagle closed his eyes and fell with his talons deep inside of the maiden. They rolled through the air and landed with full force into the roaring Rio Grande. The cliffs on both sides of the river enveloped them. The water washed them over rocks.

Life started throbbing back into them. The current of the water kept pushing them down. Mother Earth tried to grasp them out of the river, but it was too fast a current for her. Mother Earth threw up large dams to block the river. The river rushed over them and heaved the eagle and the maiden down, over, and out.

Moon shook his head and snakes fell down into the river. They guided the eagle and the maiden along. The snakes blanketed their bodies, twisting them away from the rocks and the banks of dirt which Mother Earth kept pushing forth. The maiden was guided down with the eagle. The moon's brightness began to fade. Sun shone his long warm fingers over the edge of Mother Earth. Moon moved slowly across the sky then rolled on his side and fell out of sight.

Sun illuminated Father Sky, who awoke and looked down on Mother Earth. He saw her frantically trying to stop the maiden and the eagle. The river pushed and pulled away from her. Father Sky pushed the clouds aside. The sun commanded his heat against the river. The water slowed and the snakes crawled up on shore and slithered to cold damp hiding quarters. The river eased its pulsating motion and fell into an easy slumber. The maiden reached for a rock and carefully pulled herself up. The eagle, wet and limp from exhaustion, scratched at a rock, tumbled and fell back into the water. Father Sky's long rays reached down and lifted up the wet bird. Father Sky put the bird on the shore and wrapped him in a blanket of gold.

The maiden shivered. Mother Earth reached out to her. A rock path pushed up leading to shore. The maiden carefully crawled on her hands and knees to the opposite shore of the eagle. The eagle clawed and tried to get out of the blanket. He let out a harsh loud scream. The maiden looked at the poor creature, her once captor. His scream of pain filled her with wonder. She shook her long hair dry in the hot sun. Father Sky held still. She carefully crept across the river to the rock, looking at the eagle.

Mother Earth erupted a spray of water into her face, trying to discourage her. The maiden shook her head and continued to search for a way to the eagle. Mother Earth let the rock roll off its base and float over to the shore. The maiden ran to the bird. It was now still. Its eyes were closed, its beak open, its claws bloody. A tear rolled down the maiden's face. The beautiful big bird was still, unmoving. She unrolled the blanket and lifted it up to the sun. The maiden reached up as high as her arms would and with tears rolling down her face gave a silent prayer, 'Sai-ya, ya, ya, to be free'.

Sun shook his head and golden drops of light flew around her hand, around the eagle, around the blanket and burned her eyes. She dropped the eagle rubbing her eyes. Gold drops flew everywhere. She covered her face and tried to walk away. She turned to see where the bird had landed afraid of stepping on it. There in front of her stood a magnificent man. His eyes glared at her. The gold drops faded and fell into the earth. The man's long hair blew across his face. His hands were bound around the wrist with gold thread, from these threads were fingers cut and jagged dripping with blood.

"You have taken my freedom. You have turned me into an animal that cannot fly. You were warned by the wind. I tried to take you away where you could not harm me, but Father Sky is your Father and he will not let me harm you." The tall man looked down on her. His glare was frightening. His stance firm. The maiden felt the fear come back into her being. She stepped back from him. "I can not hurt you and you are free to go." He fell on his knees and started to cry. He covered his face with his bloody fingers. She had felt the pain from his creation, and she had known the feeling of grief.

The maiden walked away and carefully crossed the river on a rock path. She pulled herself up to a ledge on a cliff and looked up at Father Sky. "Sai-ya, ya, ya."

The man's words were unclear to her. His sadness and pain were not. The maiden looked down at the man, his feelings were cold toward her. She climbed up the cliff and worked her way out of the canyon onto a plateau. She glanced at the man so small, and sad, and ran fast away from him. She ran and ran, feeling her heart and lungs almost burst from the pain. She ran across the meadow and finally found a resting place against a tree near a spring.

The sun worked its way across the sky and laid down to rest. Moon came up, he was smaller this night in his power. The maiden slept.

Wind blew dirt into a large pile near her tree. The maiden slept on. The sunshine from the sun did not awaken the maiden. Her body was tired and her eyes shut tight. The wind continued to blow, it tossed her hair. The maiden did not stir. The pile of dirt near her blew into a small mound. Neither the sun nor the moon could awaken the maiden and she slept on through days and nights, the mound next to her rising up. Mother Earth gave a sigh of relief, her creation was safe and asleep. The mound grew and began to breathe in the earth. Wind was tossing the maiden's hair wildly and blowing into her face.

Father Sky covered the earth with his black blanket and the moon slivered its way across the sky. The sun rose on this day hard and strong. The maiden stirred, she opened her eyes and looked around her, stretching her legs. The dirt mound near the tree heaved. The maiden quickly stood up and hid behind the tree. The mound heaved again, snorted, and erupted with a ferocious noise.

There in front of her was a tremendous creature. He was a four leg-ged creature, his head was wider than the tree she was standing behind. His feet were hard and pounded the earth. The ground below her rumbled with his weight. His back was broad and heavy. Four thick legs held him off the ground. His eyes were of fire, his breath smoke, and his skin was covered with a glowing fur. The maiden saw that he was stuck. The animal snorted and pulled, heaving and pulling at something behind.

The maiden silently walked to the creature. He turned his massive head and glared at her, his body sweating and shaking. The maiden carefully reached down to the ground where a long rope was held firmly in the ground. She gave it a jerk, feathers flew up from the rope and hit her across the face. She fell back and the creature burst for-ward and thundered across the plain. The maiden stood up and clap-ped her hands with pleasure. As the animal ran, large thick horns ap-peared across his forehead. The creature snorted and charged at trees and shrubs. He felled them with his mighty horns and strong forehead. His feet pounded the ground. His thunder rolled out over the plains. The maiden watched with delight at his power.

The beast now tired and quiet walked heavily over to her. He stop-ped a distance off and turned his head from side to side thinking of her. She reached out her hand to him. This ferocious beast snorted, his eyes full of wonder.

"Sai-ya, ya, ya," she said.

She put one foot in front of the other as she walked to him. He put his head down. The long rope with feathers switching back and forth behind him. She put her hand under his nose and stood still. The beast turned his head away from her. She saw his eyes smile. His nose sniffed, a long pink tongue came out of his foaming mouth and caressed the back of her hand. She pulled her hand away gently. She stroked his long bangs that hung down from the horns. His fur was soft and his temperament could be quieted. She looked at his large eyes, he was anxious to go with her.

They walked across the plain and into the green grasslands near the mountains, past the hills and down to the river. The large beast felt his way down to the river's edge. He drank, lapping the water up with his long, pink, rough tongue. Thirst was in the maiden's throat, fear was still very clearly implanted in her mind. She searched the river and the shore for the man. She saw nothing, she listened, and heard nothing except the slurping of the beast.

She placed her hand on the back of the beast. His long rope with the feathers on it started to jerk back and forth. The maiden reached down into the water. Her hand touched the surface, as her fingers submerged into the water, snakes crawled up her hand. She screamed and pulled away. The snakes came out of the water grabbing at her ankles. They were still trying to wrap themselves around her as Moon had ordered them. She struggled for her freedom away from them. The beast stamped his hooves, the vibration scared many of them back into the water. The beast rubbed against the maiden, she grabbed his long flowing hair around his neck. The beast braced his feet against the firm ground and yanked the maiden free. She was flung across his back. The beast charged up the hill and onto the grasslands. Her eyes filled with tears as the air flew by her. The ground swiftly disappeared under the great beast's feet. The beast ran around and around the grasslands. As he ran the snakes fell off onto the ground. The maiden pulled herself up and straddled the beast. He charged up and down the hills, mountains, and open ranges.

The maiden laughed and stroked the beast, his heaving body sweating and snorting below her. She felt his power. The power she had lost to the eagle returned to her. She knew now what freedom was.

The beast roamed the hills. The maiden fell asleep on his broad back. Her hair floated down to his long legs as he walked. The sun slipped down the other side of a mountain and Father Sky covered the earth with his black blanket. He peered down at her through the holes he had made for that purpose and saw the maiden slip down off the beast and quietly fall to the ground. The maiden dug a small nook and fell asleep once again.

The beast stamped his feet. The maiden awoke. She moved her arms, the beast's nostrils were flaring, his eyes set, and his mane blowing in the wind. There was something out there. The maiden turned her head and listened. Footsteps moved towards them. The maiden jumped up and ran to the side of the beast. She felt the ground shake, the sound became louder. The heavy plodding on the ground was coming from the direction the beast was looking in. The long rope with the feathers slowly swishing back and forth.

The beast moved out of the trees, his breathing slow and quiet. His fat ears upright. There on the horizon was an image walking towards them. The ground shook, the image became clear. It was another beast. This one was smaller, had less fur, and did not have horns. The big beast let out a long loud bellow. The smaller beast stopped, laughing with short grunts. The big beast turned and looked at the maiden. He nudged her with his nose, his eyes full of fire. The maiden patted his soft nose. She knew that it was time for him to leave. "Sai-ya, ya, you are free."

The big beast lifted his large feet and galloped up to the smaller beast. He charged at her. She turned and ran from him. Then the smaller beast turned and waited for him. The big beast threw his head back and bellowed, the two of them ran off side by side out of the maiden's sight. All that was left was floating dust.

The maiden put her hands down. She was alone. She looked around for some food, her stomach talking to her. There was nothing around but the trees. The longer she had been away from water, the more she realized that she needed it. She pushed her long hair back, walked forward toward the river, holding her hand over her chest. It hurt painfully. She felt a pain that one could not see. The beast was gone. She rubbed her chest hard, trying to remove the pain. It remained but she kept walking.

The sun was low in the sky when she reached a small stream. There were bones all around it. She lifted up one of the bones. It was white and turned to powder in her hand. It smelled of burned grass. She dropped it in the water and saw the ripples slowly fade to the edge.

She bent over the water and looked in. There was her own reflection. Her hair tangled around her neck, her eyes large and dark, her mouth dry and sore. The water rippled again without her moving.

She watched again the ripples move out, the reflection was different. Behind her stood a man. She jumped and reached for a rock. A hand held her arm. She could not move. The man pushed her hair away from her face, he touched her cheek. He grabbed her arms and flung her across his back. She kicked, screaming, pulling his hair, biting his back. He dropped her on the ground. "You are coming with me. Either I can hit you very hard and carry you like a dead animal or you can come with me willingly."

The maiden pulled her manta back across her shoulder, pushed up her bracelets, and stood straight beside him. She glanced forward, he walked ahead of her. She followed him. They walked from the plain into the canyons. Up the canyons into a valley and before her were a group of people all living high up on the cliffs, in caves with wood shelters outside the doors. The people watched her, talking among themselves.

"Remember that you are with me. You will not be hurt if you stay close. There are men here who may try to grab you or hurt you. I am a brave hunter and most of the men here are afraid of me. Stay close and do not try to run."

The man pulled her in front of him. She looked at him with his strange glazed eyes. These people were different and she knew that they in turn knew that she was different. Her necklaces banged against her chest as she walked. She remembered the weight of them when the eagle had lifted her off the ground. She remembered the eagle telling her that Father Sky would take care of her. She lifted her head to look up, the man pushed her head down and she fell forward.

"Do not look around or you will get the people's attention. Just walk ahead. We are almost there." She kept her head down and walked on. He jerked her aside and pulled her up along a path. They were at the base of a cliff. He pointed to the footholes and she climbed up. He pushed her into a cave.

The cave was dark and full of smoke. Her eyes watered. She heard a woman's voice singing toward the back of the cave. She moved around the fire and sat down. The cave was filled with baskets, blankets, dolls, bowls with different things in them, and a wooden cradle board. The man watched her and shook his head. Tears ran down his face. He whispered softly toward the back of the cave. A woman came out. She had covered her face with black dust, her clothes were covered with dirt, she was also crying. The man held her in his arms. She pulled away and reached for the maiden. The maiden pulled back afraid. These people were very strange. She had not seen persons like herself before, except the eagle man. They were acting very strangely. The woman knelt and reached for the maiden's hand. "Our child, she is dead. We waited and waited to have a child. Now she is gone. She was just new, we hardly had time to know her. The Spirits have taken her from us. The wise man told us of you. You can help us. Please do not be afraid, we need your help and we will not hurt you." She buried her face in her hands. The maiden touched the woman on the shoulder and pointed to the back of the cave.

"Go and get the child for her," the woman spoke harshly to the man. He disappeared. The pain in the woman's face was a pain that the maiden knew. It hurt in the chest. It was a pain that would not go away and that no one could see.

The man returned with a bundle. The blanket was torn on the sides. He opened it kneeling in front of the maiden. She pushed back the blanket, there lay a beautiful child.

The maiden touched the cheek of the child. She did not move. The child's eyes were open and her mouth was swollen. There were red marks all over the child's body. The man screamed and pulled away from them. He grabbed some hot charcoal from the fire and started rubbing it all over his face. The maiden put her hand up to her lips. They were all quiet. The maiden took the bundle outside and held it up to the sun. The blanket moved, the child breathed, an eagle flew out of the blanket. The woman clutched the blanket. It was empty. She threw the blanket over the cliff, the wind picked it up and blew away with it. The woman turned to the maiden who was standing there smiling. She had never known that she had such magic. The woman embraced her. Now their child's spirit was free.

The woman fixed a big feast for them. They sat around the fire until the cliffs were quiet and Father Sky had put his blanket around Mother Earth. The maiden wanted to leave. She did not want to stay in the cave with the smoke burning her eyes, or the feeling of death still heavy in the walls. She waited until the first light of the sun. She fled down the cliff and away to the south of the cliff caves. She ran with great speed. She turned her head to see if anyone was following her.

As she turned her foot caught onto a rope. She pulled with her hands and they in turn were caught up in this sticky rope. She fell backward and was completely stuck. The ropes went all the way up the side of a cliff and to a cave opening. She called out. "Sai-ya, ya, ya, free me."

Out of the cave came an old woman with a spear. She floated down the ropes and came swiftly to the maiden. She held the spear up high, ready for the kill. The maiden put her hand out and cried up to Father Sky. The old woman smiled through her yellow teeth. She laughed and poked the maiden. The maiden lifted her eyes and reached her free hand up to the sky. The ground started to shake. The woman looked around her. Her long torn black dress caught in the ropes. She bent down to pull it free.

The ground rumbled as with thunder. The old woman looked up just as the beast came charging through the ropes. He broke everything in his path with his huge horns. He ran straight for her. The old woman now standing upright held the spear out to meet the beast head on. The beast lowered his head and with a loud snort threw her up into the air. She seemed to fly tumbling over and over and then she hit the ground. The old woman smashed into a hundred little spiders which ran in every direction away from the beast.

The beast turned and galloped to the maiden. She mounted his back and he bellowed, his head tossing the remainder of the rope on the ground. He ran and ran over the ground until he came back to the trees on the plain. The maiden had fallen asleep being gently rocked by the movement of the beast, her long hair hanging down to his long legs.

The moon came up and shone with splendor on the maiden gently being rocked. The beast stopped weary of his long trek. The maiden fell to the ground and curled up fast asleep. She slept through days and nights. Her dreams reminding her of the things that had happened and the fears that were still around her.

A hand touched her shoulder. Her eyes did not open. The hand pushed gently the long hair from her face. Her breathing remained steady and soft. The hand shook her gently. The maiden moved her feet. The hand touched her back and began to rub softly. The maiden jumped, the beast was gone. The maiden carefully moved on her side, turned on her knee looking right into the face of a man. This man she knew. He was the eagle man. Her bracelets were laying beside her. Her necklace was in her lap. She froze staring at him bewildered. The man looked at her with a smile. His hands were still bound with gold, his face was no longer stern, his eyes were solemn, but now he appeared to be friendly.

He did not speak to her. He pushed her hair back from her face and handed her some berries. She grabbed them and ate. He pulled a leather pouch from his belt with water dripping from it. She reached for it and he gave it to her. She wiped the water from her manta, it was torn. There was blood on her knee and her feet were without her white moccasins. Her moccasins were lying next to the eagle man. They had turned a deep brown-red. She grabbed them and rubbed. They shone as she rubbed, but they would not turn white. What had happened while she slept? What had happened as she dreamt of flying and soaring for freedom? The eagle man stood up and walked away. He limped badly, his knees too were covered with blood. He bent down and threw a dead snake away from them.

She stood up and stretched her long legs. She was sore and tired. The man walked towards the river. She followed him. He sat down under a tree and motioned for her to sit with him. She did with some caution. He put his arm around her and kissed her in the same manner as the man in the cave to his woman. She remembered the beast and his wet pink rough tongue. She relaxed in the man's arms. The man put his hand on her stomach and rubbed. The maiden smiled, she relaxed and slept until late night.

The man would go to the river at night for water. The snakes were not around during the night. He showed her where the berries were growing. They caught small fish from the river by building a dam in the night. He cooked them under a fire of pinons. The days passed into many. She knew how good it felt to eat well and to no longer be afraid. She worked side by side with the eagle man. At times she would look at his hands and feel fear. So she decided not to look at them and think more of his calm warmth.

They worked hard at night building a mud house. They gathered water and made a mud hollow. During the day they would scoop it up with their hands and pat it into place. It was not very large, the rain washed away their work at times. The eagle man had incredible strength, he would work all day and well into the night. The mud house moved ahead despite the rain storms and the walls became tall enough for them to walk next to without bending down. The roof they made out of strips of dead wood, laced with green strips of cedar. The roof was finished just before the first snowfall. The fire had to be built in the door opening, for the smoke inside would drive them out with choking coughs and weeping eyes.

The cold weather brought a new feeling to the maiden. She groaned in the cold. She had trouble getting up and down from the little mud house to the hills below. The maiden's feet would ache after a long walk. The eagle man brought her food, built warm fires, and began to weave. She noticed his weaving had begun when she became fat. She was getting fatter and fatter. Food disgusted her and the idea of becoming fat and not eating brought on the long forgotten hunger. The maiden became weak and tired. She slept through the days. Her face grew pale. The wind continued to blow.

The maiden reached out. She grabbed the eagle man by the hand. He was sleeping close to her, to help keep her warm. She pulled his arm around her. She placed his hand on her huge belly. He moved closer to her. Something inside of her was moving. It was moving a lot. The eagle man gave her a tight hug and laughed. This moving thing kicked her and fought with her a lot.

The next day, the wind stopped blowing. The man lifted her up and took her outside. The sun shone down on her. Her face glowed with the warmth. The cold white snow stopped coming and the world was at peace. She continued to grow fat. This thing inside of her kept kicking her. The eagle man was happy with her moving belly. The maiden was afraid of it. This thing inside of her fought hard battles with her when she tried to sleep. If she tried to walk very far it would kick her violently until she had to sit down. This thing would have to leave her body and give her some peace. She did not feel that she wanted it inside of her, but she was not sure what she would have to do with it once it was outside of her belly.

The eagle man continued to weave the basket. It was small and oval. He pulled spring field grass and lined it with soft down from birds. The gold threads still bound his hands. She would look down at the gold threads weaving the basket, stopping and rubbing her belly, then touching her hands. The hands that were once red and bloody were now rubbing her. She became unsure of herself. She looked to Father Sky and hoped that he would answer all of her questions.

One morning she felt a cold come up her legs. Her feet grew numb. She cried out. There was no one to hear her, for the eagle man was in the plain gathering some grass. She reached forward and tried to stand up. Pain pierced through her body. She pulled herself up and leaned on the door. The door of the mud house cracked under her weight and started to crumble. She fell forward, screaming again and again. Her head hurt and her eyes closed.

Large hands carried her inside. Water dripped down her forehead. Her mouth was dry and her throat hurt. The eagle man was there. He held her rocking back and forth singing. This was the first time that she had heard his voice since their first meeting. He rocked her, stopping to put a wet cloth on her forehead. She reached out for the water. He pulled it away from her. She glared at him and struggled for it. He threw the water on the mud house. He laid her down on the straw mat. He pushed her hair up and away from her face. He started to undress her. She grabbed his hands. The gold threads were gone. She pushed her heavy body away from him. He kept pulling at her manta. She kicked dirt in his face. She had to be free from his hands. He fell back. She crawled on her hands and knees out into the sun. She reached up her hands to Father Sky.

The eagle man stood in the dwelling, he did not follow her out into the sunlight. The maiden groaned with pain. The man started out towards her, then stopped. He would not come out into the sunlight. He stood watching her, wringing his hands. He started yelling at her, she did not hear him. She crawled on her knees and hands to the water pouch. She poured the cold water into her mouth and lay back in the sun. The eagle man could no longer see her, she was now behind a group of trees. He started wailing and crying.

The maiden pulled herself up and over an embankment. She could see him pulling at his hair and crying. The pain engulfed her body. She remembered the first pain that she had ever felt. He had brought that on her, too. She fell back and waited for the pain to stop. It came again and again harder and harder. She cried out and called up to Father Sky. He beamed down with the sun. She cried for Mother Earth to help her. There was no reply. She closed her eyes and breathed with the coming and going of the pain.

This thing inside of her kicked and fought its way through her body, turning and pushing, wriggling and pulsating toward its exit. She pushed and heaved, the pain shot through her body until she no longer felt any pain. The thing was out of her at last. The man was screaming and walking back and forth, beating at his head with his fists. The maiden sat up and looked at the thing. It did not move. She rubbed it hard and poked at it. The thing began to squirm. The maiden put her fingers on its shiny covering and piece by piece pulled the covering off.

Father Sky shook his head and golden drops fell from the sky covering the thing and her hands. The man could no longer stand it, he ran out to her. The maiden pulled herself up ready for him. Brother Sun reached down and lifted the man up and he flew off in the shape of an eagle. The maiden watched him soar around her and then up and out of view. She squinted as the gold drops around the thing became brighter and brighter. The thing began to move more and more. It too wanted its freedom. She moved back and away from it. The thing began to shake and move. The gold drops around it settled. The eagle came back flying low in the sky and straight for them. The maiden fell on the ground. The eagle swooped down and picked up the thing.

He carried it up high into the sky. He soared up, up, and became a spot high above her. Then he dropped the thing. It fell with a great speed. As it fell closer to earth the maiden could hear the horrible whistling sound it made. The eagle swooped down and picked it up again in his beak. He lifted it up again and let go. The thing fell again towards Mother Earth. Then it suddenly began to soar. It flew high above the maiden. The eagle and the baby eagle soared around and around her head. She looked up and smiled clapping her hands. The eagle was now free from the bondage of Mother Earth. The maiden was now free from the bondage of the eagle man and the thing.

The maiden, tired and weak, sat down and watched the two birds fly through the sky. She slept for many days. Her dreams reminded her of what had happened and of the fears that she had in her life. The moon rose that night and cast a light hue over the land. On the edge of the cliff high on a mountain in a small cave was a large eagle sleeping with its wing around a smaller new eagle. A beast large and ferocious was quietly breathing with a smaller beast. The large beast with the feet of thunder now had feathers growing on his chest. His smaller beasts slept curled up on the ground behind him. He perked up his ears to hear the sound of a baby crying off in the distance from the cliff dwellings. The river ran freely nearby and a gentle wind blew.

The maiden slept on and on. Her body relaxing as the days moved on. The wind blew small bits of dirt around her. Father Sky looked down on her during the day and noticed the mound growing larger and larger. Mother Earth, one night while the moon was but a sliver, engulfed her creation in her arms. The moon rolled over and fell out of sight to the morning sun. All that was left was a large mound around a lone pinon tree on the plain.

She shuffled out into the blowing storm. Her shawls wrapped around her. The old lady disappeared into the white blowing wind.

AFTERWORD

The men worked slowly without hesitation. The wiring would not be finished before lunch. The store was inches deep in ladders, sawdust, cigarette butts, and foul language. There was no knock at the side door, perhaps tomorrow.

The potbellied stove sat in its place all day with people walking around it, bumping into it, and not noticing it. The store echoed in hollowness as the day wore on. Little ones came in for candy. Older men came in for their cigarettes. Women came in for the herbs. Uncle Tito came in for his toilet paper and dog food. He had the dogs wait outside. Uncle Tito watched the men work. He shook his head. He walked up to me. I was shelving soup cans.

"You are here."

"So are you."

"We are here together."

He saluted me. I saluted back.

"No story today, huh?"

I shook my head. He mumbled something and walked away. I turned to put the box back and almost knocked him down. He was rubbing apples on his pant leg. "You should shine these and more people would buy them." I nodded.

"You know that she is not from here?"

I dropped the box and watched him.

"No, she is from Spain. She came here before I was born." I smiled.

"Well, maybe not that early. She knows more than the elders. She is very wise. She married a farmer from here. She came from a strict family of Spaniards."

I picked up an apple and rubbed it on my apron.

"She is telling Indian stories to another Spaniard." Uncle Tito shook his head. He put the apple down and walked out of the store. I put my apple down and went to work in the warehouse.

The warehouse was dark and still. God, keep her well. She is doing Your work. You have done much to preserve the laws, love and traditions of the world. Please don't let these stories be lost, I silently prayed. I reached up and pulled the light string. The light swung illuminating the shelves of boxes waiting to be opened.